W9-BFC-812

GREATEST SPORTS MOMENTS

SOCCER SHOWDOWN

U.S. WOMEN'S STUNNING 1999 WORLD CUP WIN

BY BRANDON TERRELL
ILLUSTRATED BY EDUARDO GARCIA AND RED WOLF STUDIO

CONSULTANT:
BRUCE BERGLUND
PROFESSOR OF HISTORY, CALVIN COLLEGE
GRAND RAPIDS, MICHIGAN

CAPSTONE PRESS
a capstone imprint

Graphic Library is published by Capstone Press,
1710 Roe Crest Drive, North Mankato, Minnesota 56003
www.mycapstone.com

Library of Congress Cataloging-in-Publication data is available on the Library of Congress website.
ISBN 978-1-5435-4220-2 (hardcover)
ISBN 978-1-5435-4222-6 (paperback)
ISBN 978-1-5435-4224-0 (eBook PDF)

Summary: In graphic novel format, tells the dramatic story of the U.S. Women's Soccer team victory in the 1999 Women's World Cup tournament.

EDITOR
Aaron J. Sautter

ART DIRECTOR
Nathan Gassman

DESIGNER
Kyle Grenz

MEDIA RESEARCHER
Eric Gohl

PRODUCTION SPECIALIST
Katy LaVigne

Direct quotations appear in ***bold italicized text*** on the following pages:

Pages 5, 14, 15, 17, 19, 21–23, 26: from ESPN Films, *Nine for IX: The 99ers*, (https://www.youtube.com/watch?v=IWbKYAFF5Hw).
Page 7: from "Go for the Goal," by Mariel Margaret Hamm, CNN.com, July 14, 1999 (http://www.cnn.com/books/beginnings/9907/Go.For.Goal/).
Page 28: from "Women's World Cup Soccer Team," C-Span.org, July 19, 1999 (https://www.c-span.org/video/?150657-1/womens-world-cup-soccer-team).
Page 29: from "The Spirit of 1999 Women's World Cup Lives On," by Bill Plaschke, Los Angeles Times, July 10, 2009 (http://articles.latimes.com/2009/jul/10/sports/sp-plaschke10).

Printed and bound in the United States of America.
PA48

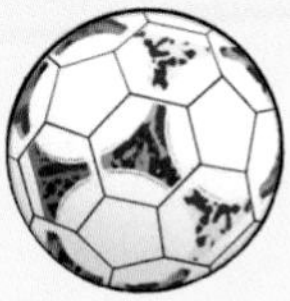

TABLE OF CONTENTS

TEAMWORK

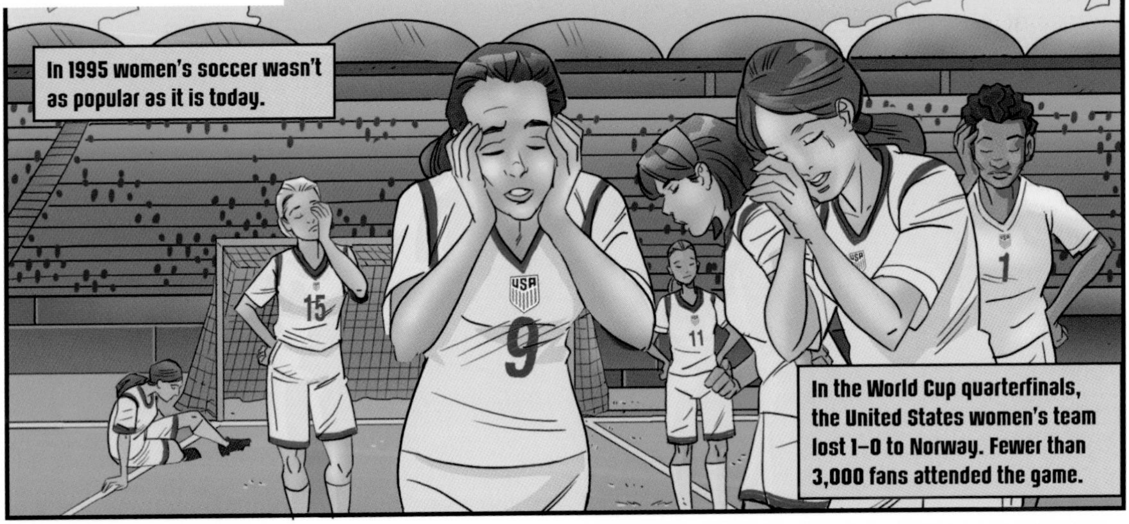
In 1995 women's soccer wasn't as popular as it is today.
In the World Cup quarterfinals, the United States women's team lost 1–0 to Norway. Fewer than 3,000 fans attended the game.

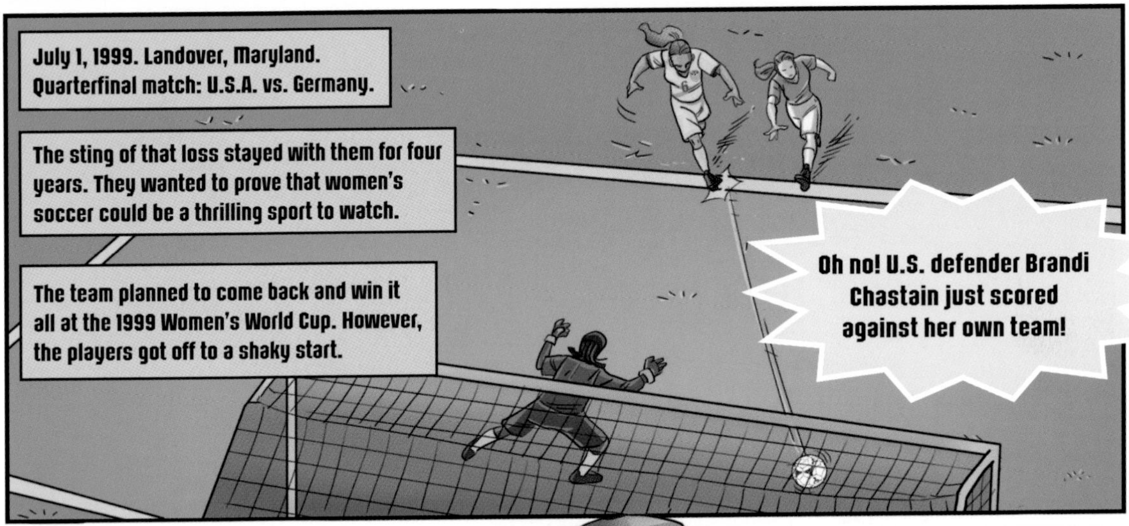
July 1, 1999. Landover, Maryland. Quarterfinal match: U.S.A. vs. Germany.
The sting of that loss stayed with them for four years. They wanted to prove that women's soccer could be a thrilling sport to watch.
The team planned to come back and win it all at the 1999 Women's World Cup. However, the players got off to a shaky start.
Oh no! U.S. defender Brandi Chastain just scored against her own team!

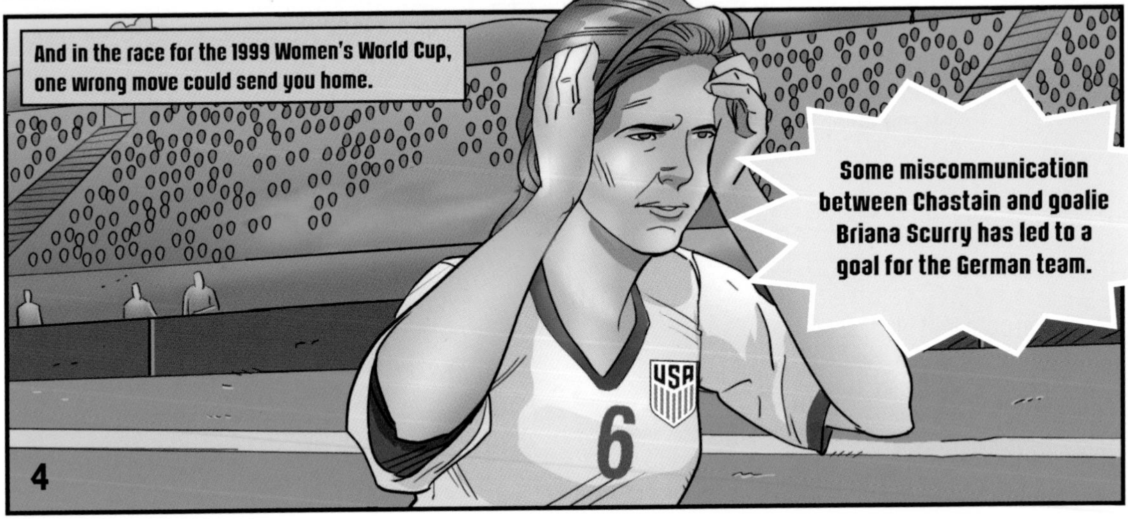
And in the race for the 1999 Women's World Cup, one wrong move could send you home.
Some miscommunication between Chastain and goalie Briana Scurry has led to a goal for the German team.

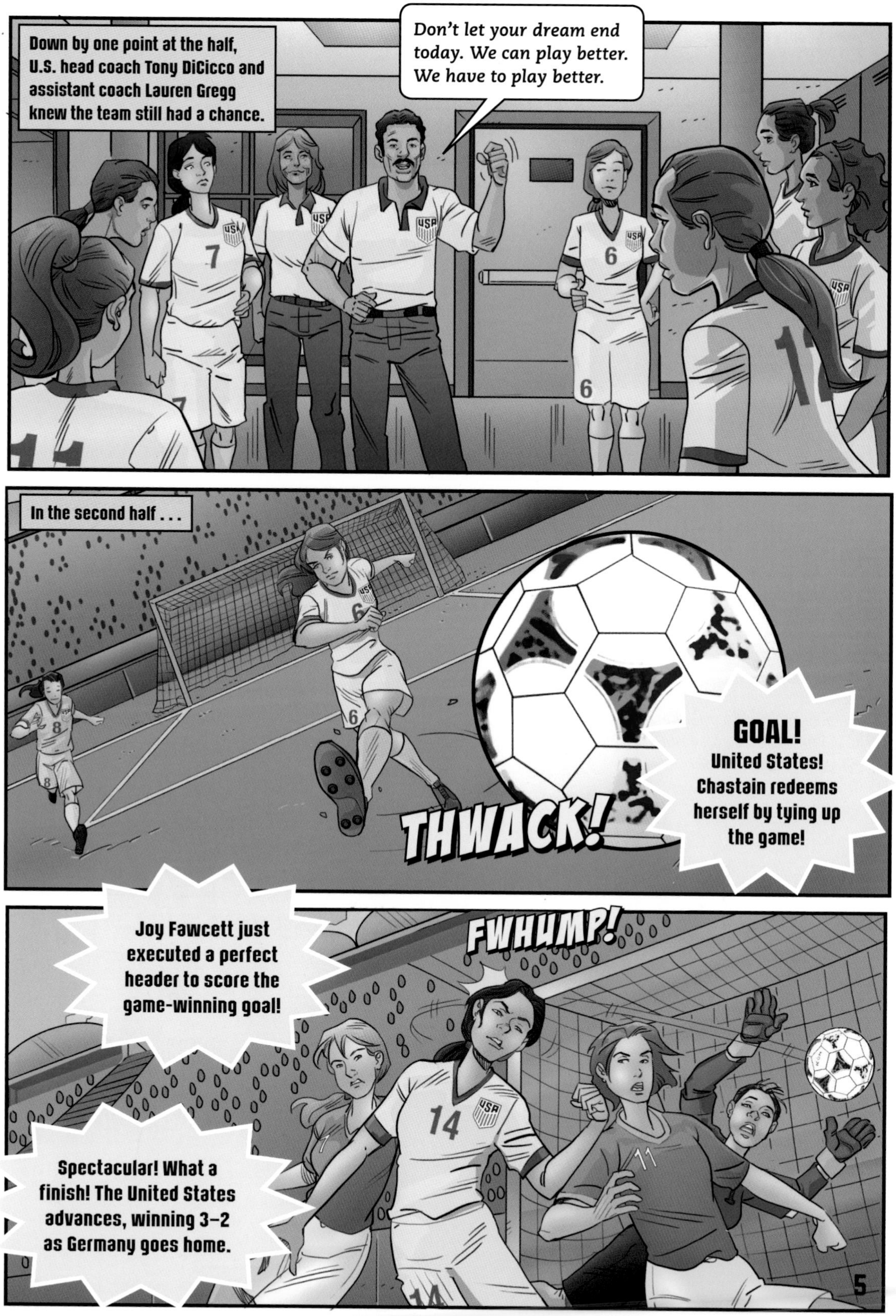
Down by one point at the half, U.S. head coach Tony DiCicco and assistant coach Lauren Gregg knew the team still had a chance.
Don't let your dream end today. We can play better. We have to play better.
In the second half . . .
THWACK!
GOAL! United States! Chastain redeems herself by tying up the game!
Joy Fawcett just executed a perfect header to score the game-winning goal!
FWHUMP!
Spectacular! What a finish! The United States advances, winning 3–2 as Germany goes home.

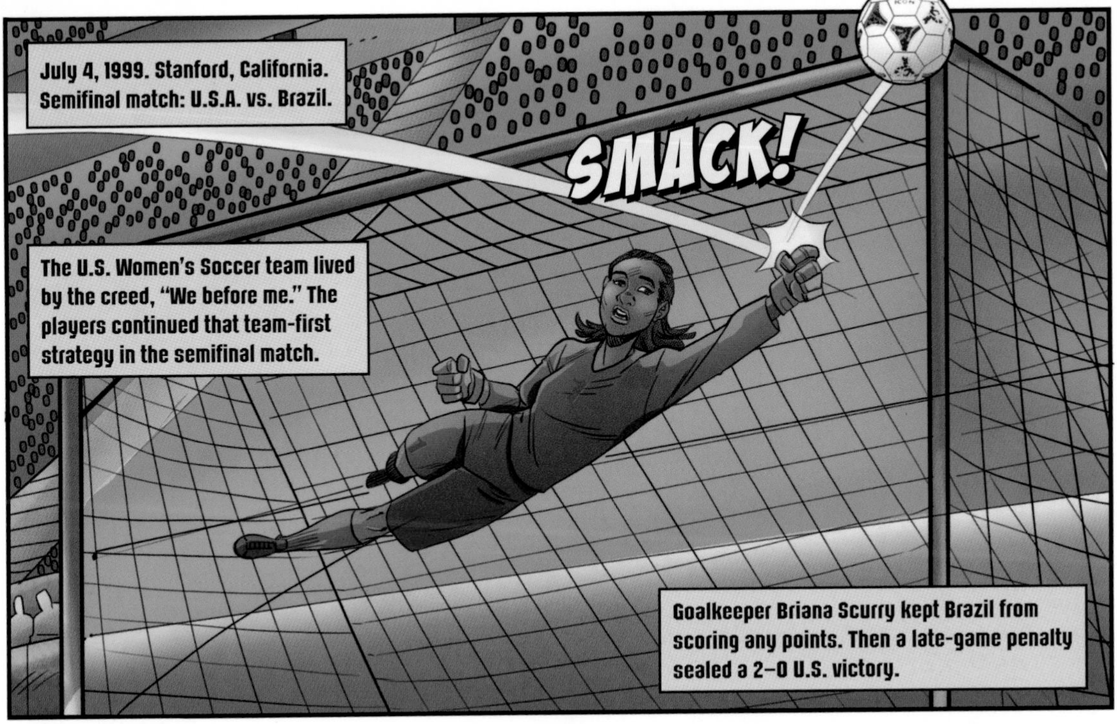
July 4, 1999. Stanford, California.
Semifinal match: U.S.A. vs. Brazil.
SMACK!
The U.S. Women's Soccer team lived by the creed, "We before me." The players continued that team-first strategy in the semifinal match.
Goalkeeper Briana Scurry kept Brazil from scoring any points. Then a late-game penalty sealed a 2–0 U.S. victory.

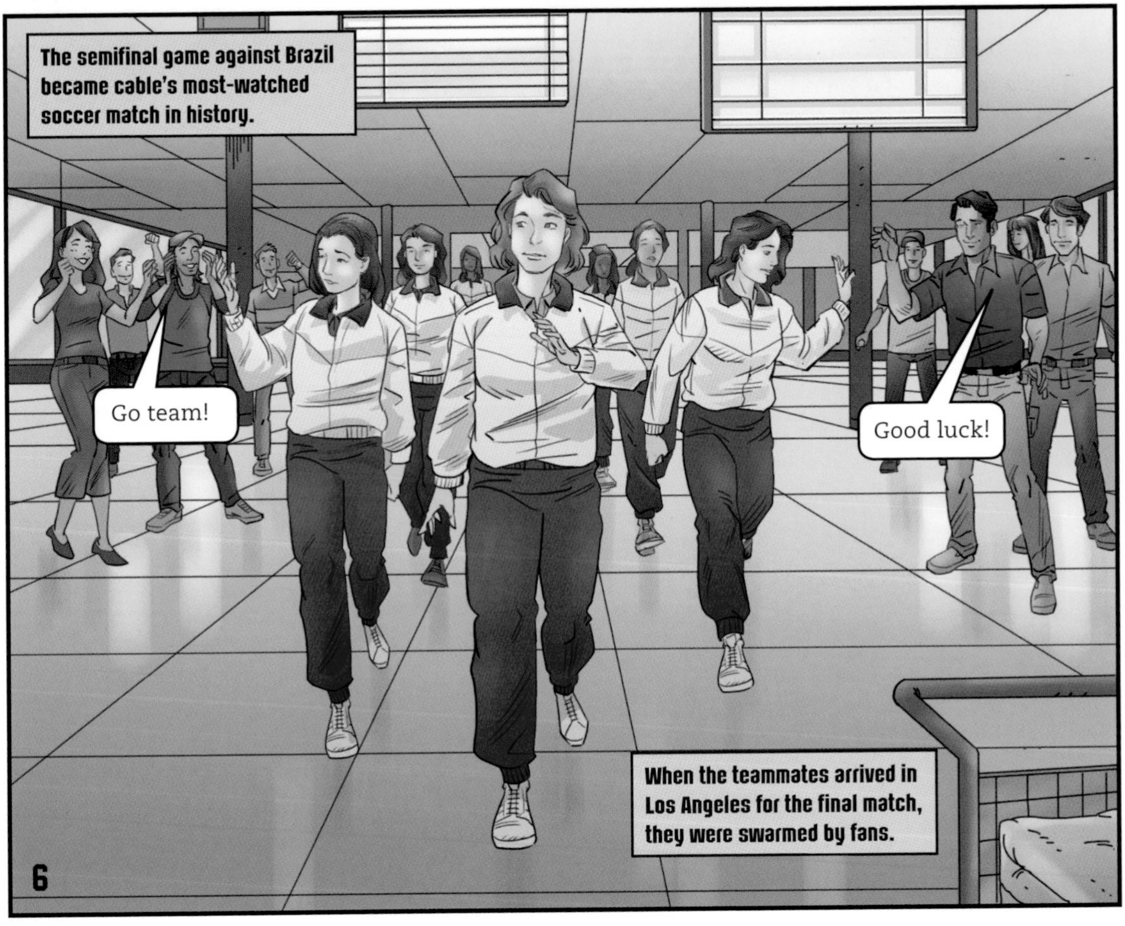
The semifinal game against Brazil became cable's most-watched soccer match in history.
Go team!
Good luck!
When the teammates arrived in Los Angeles for the final match, they were swarmed by fans.

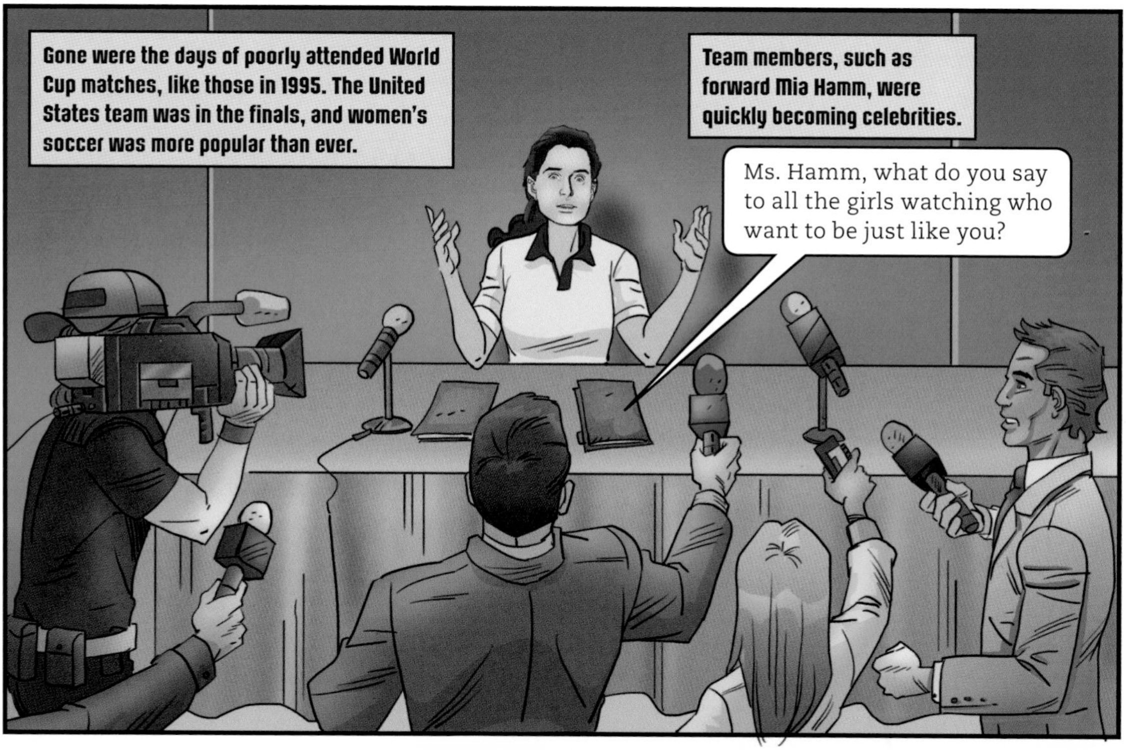
Gone were the days of poorly attended World Cup matches, like those in 1995. The United States team was in the finals, and women's soccer was more popular than ever.
Team members, such as forward Mia Hamm, were quickly becoming celebrities.
Ms. Hamm, what do you say to all the girls watching who want to be just like you?

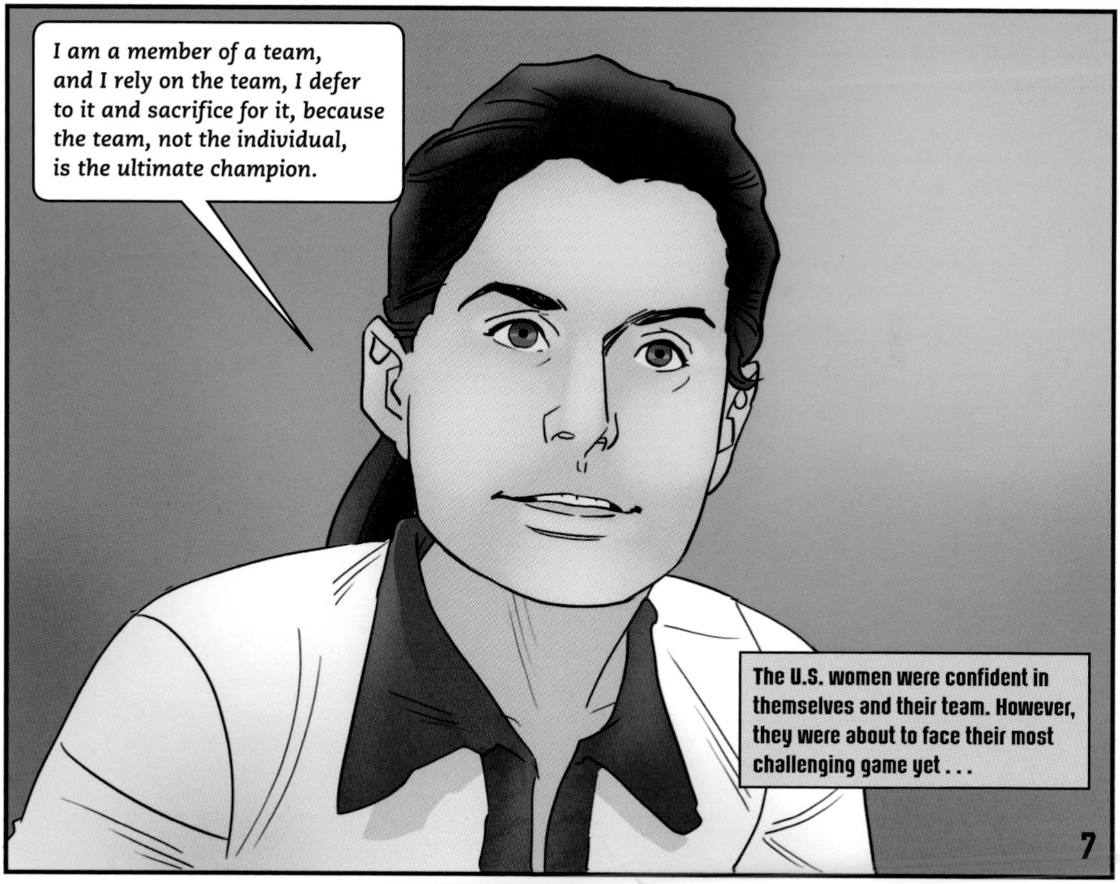
I am a member of a team, and I rely on the team, I defer to it and sacrifice for it, because the team, not the individual, is the ultimate champion.
The U.S. women were confident in themselves and their team. However, they were about to face their most challenging game yet . . .
7

THE WORLD IS WATCHING

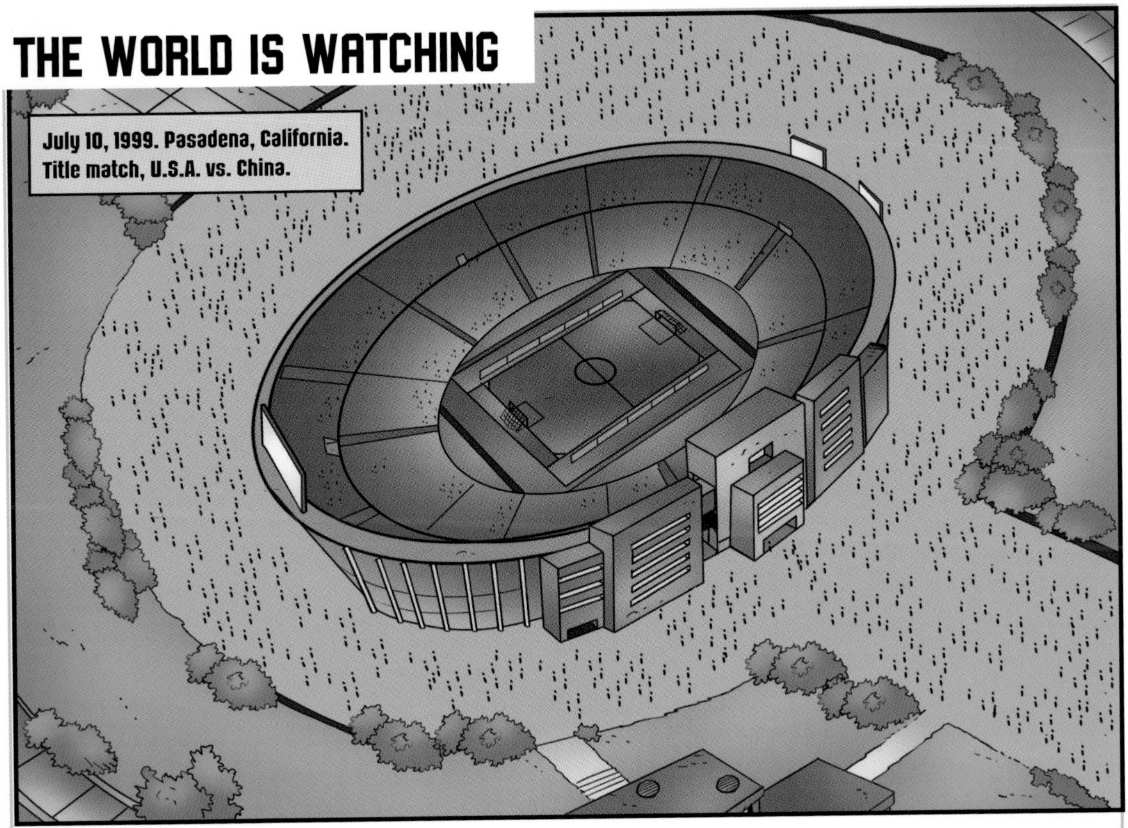
July 10, 1999. Pasadena, California.
Title match, U.S.A. vs. China.

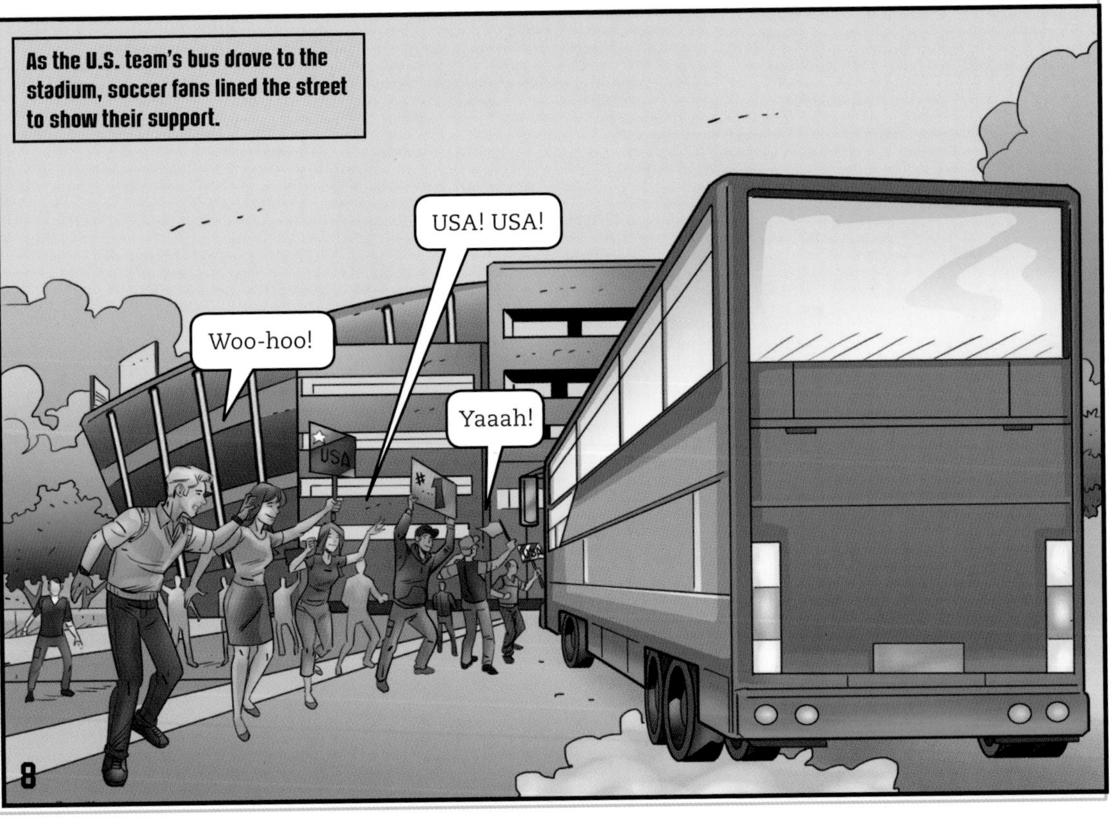
As the U.S. team's bus drove to the stadium, soccer fans lined the street to show their support.
Woo-hoo!
USA! USA!
Yaaah!
USA

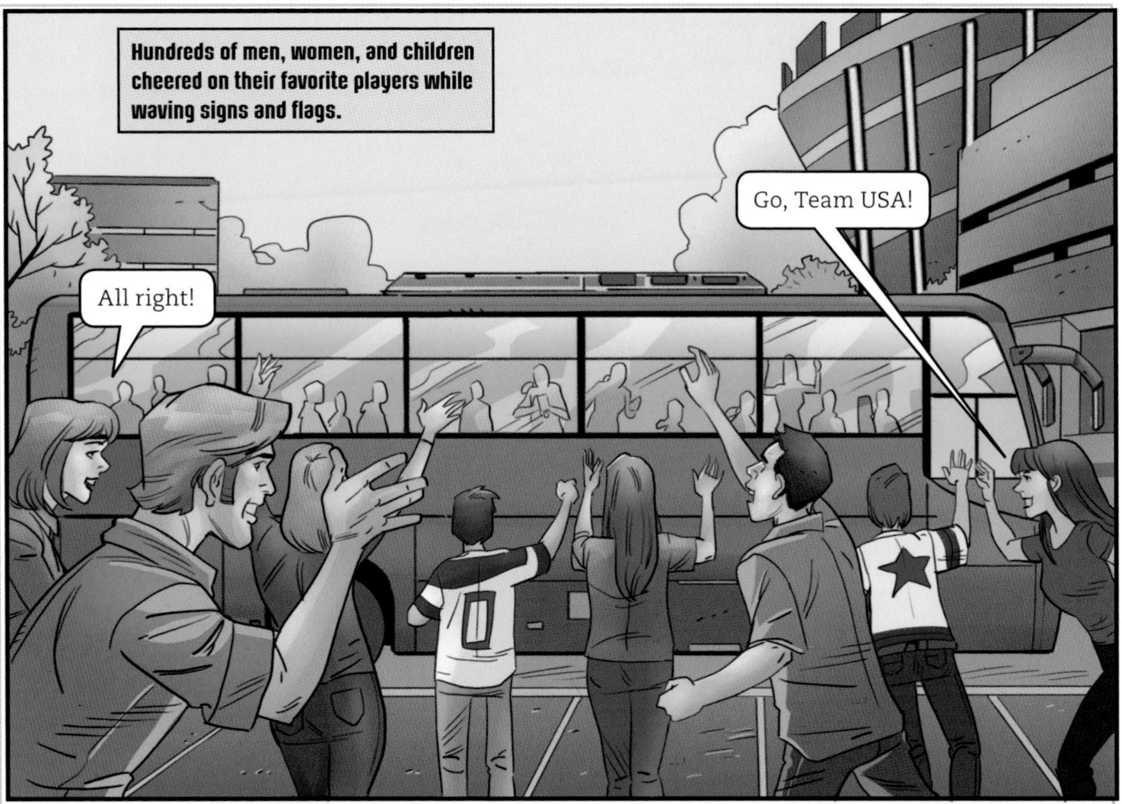
Hundreds of men, women, and children cheered on their favorite players while waving signs and flags.
All right!
Go, Team USA!

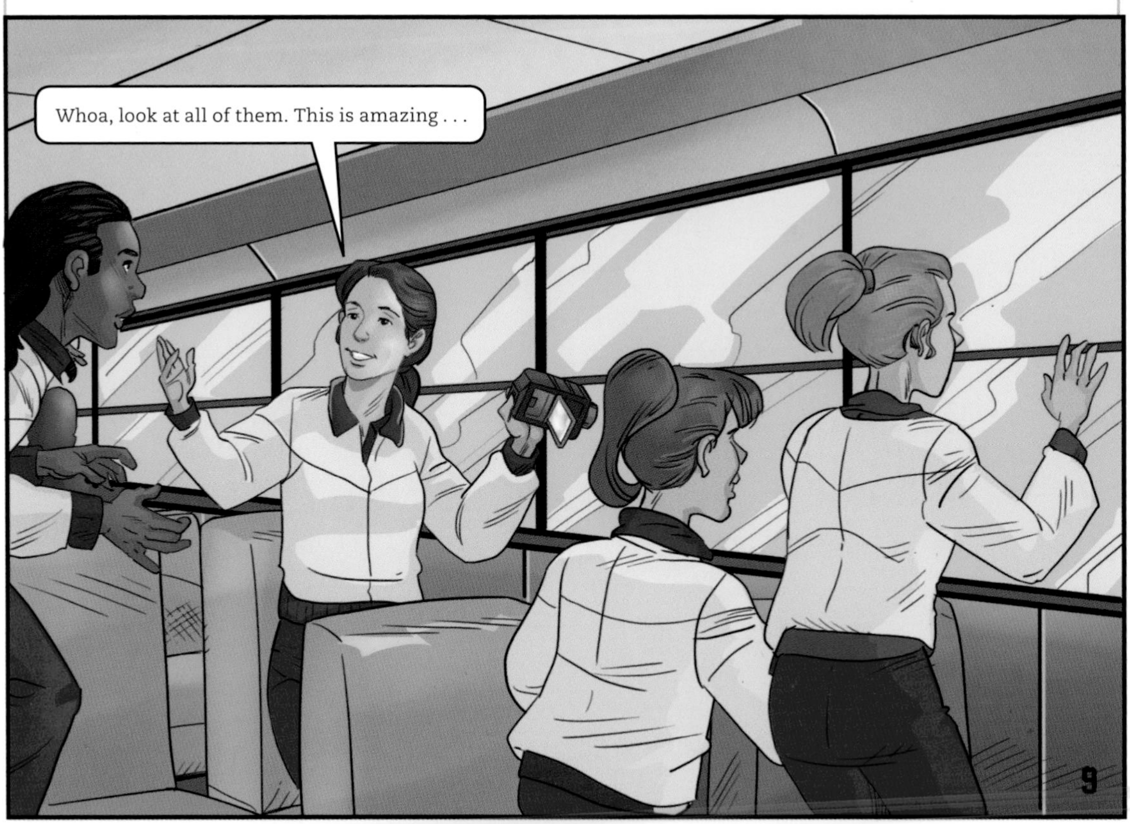
Whoa, look at all of them. This is amazing . . .

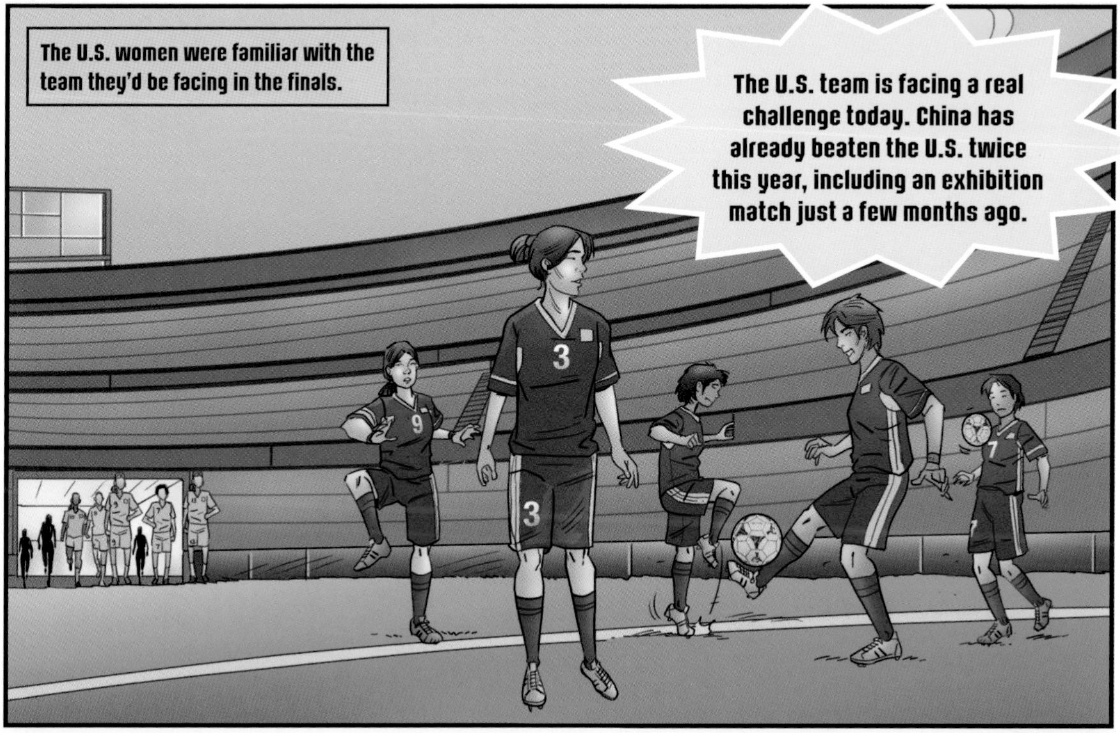
The U.S. women were familiar with the team they'd be facing in the finals.
The U.S. team is facing a real challenge today. China has already beaten the U.S. twice this year, including an exhibition match just a few months ago.

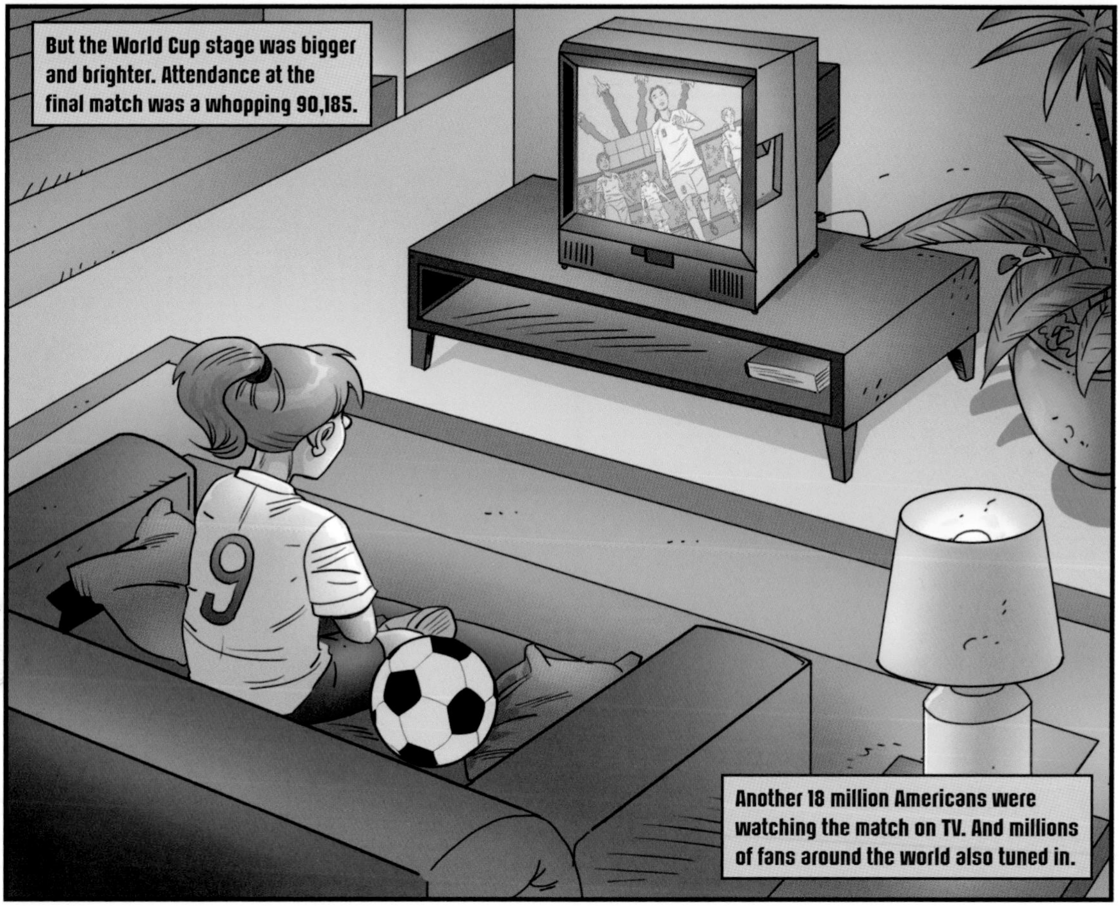
But the World Cup stage was bigger and brighter. Attendance at the final match was a whopping 90,185.
Another 18 million Americans were watching the match on TV. And millions of fans around the world also tuned in.

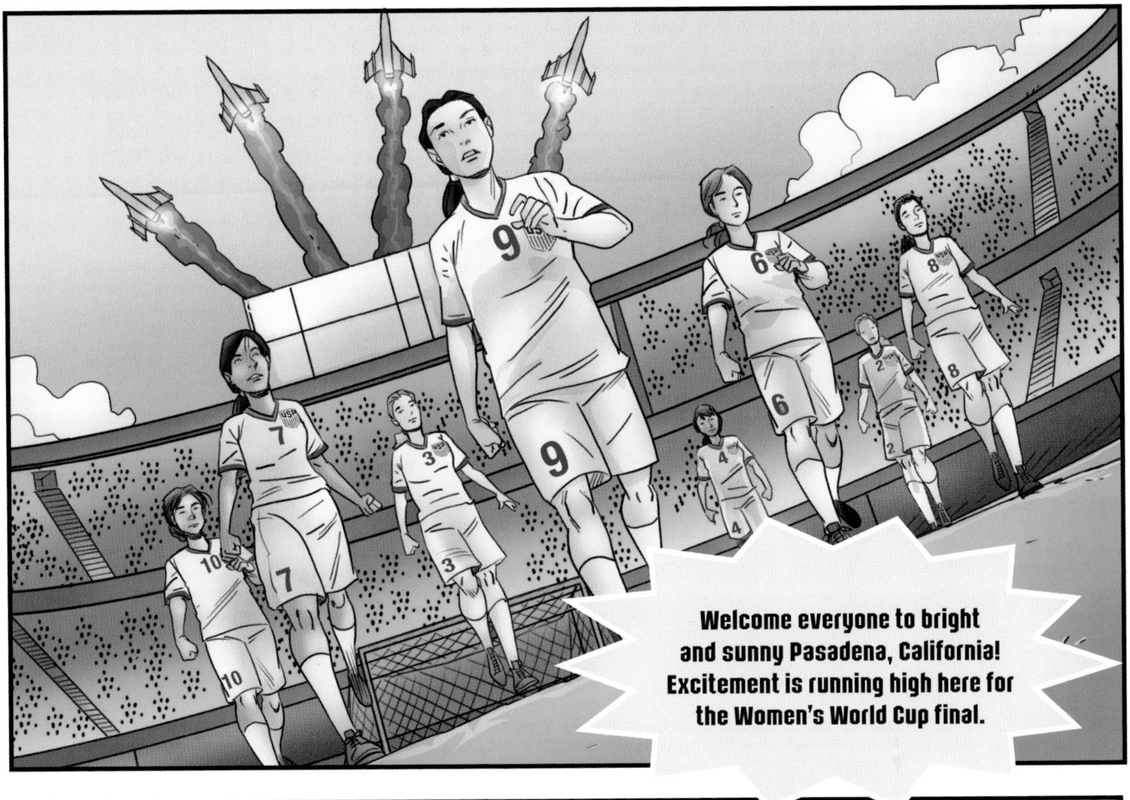
Welcome everyone to bright and sunny Pasadena, California! Excitement is running high here for the Women's World Cup final.

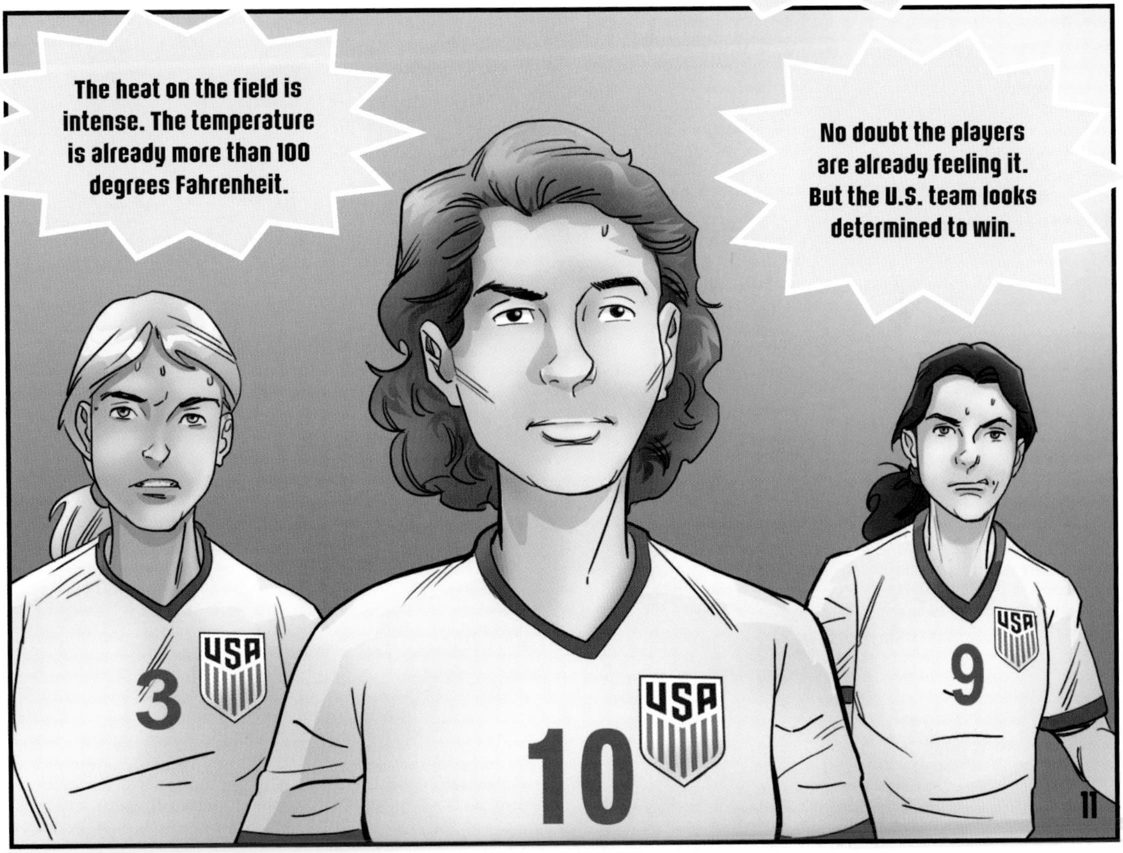
The heat on the field is intense. The temperature is already more than 100 degrees Fahrenheit.
No doubt the players are already feeling it. But the U.S. team looks determined to win.

THE HEAT IS ON

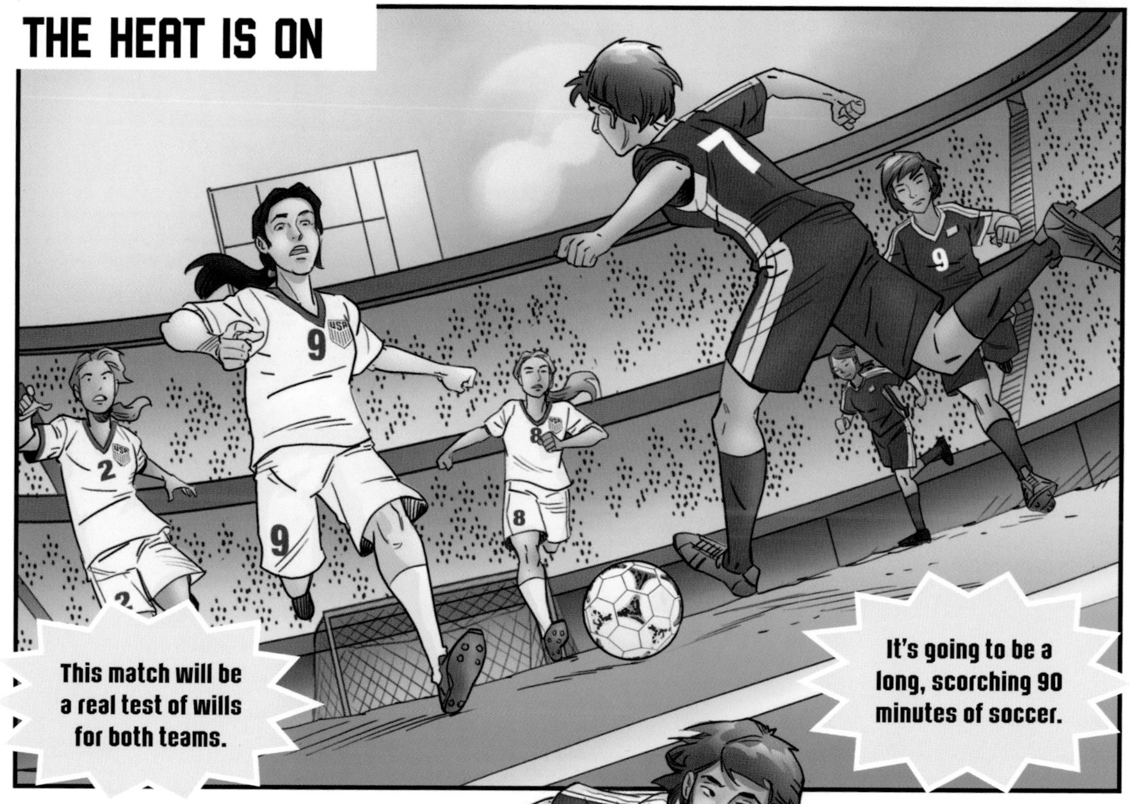
This match will be a real test of wills for both teams.
It's going to be a long, scorching 90 minutes of soccer.

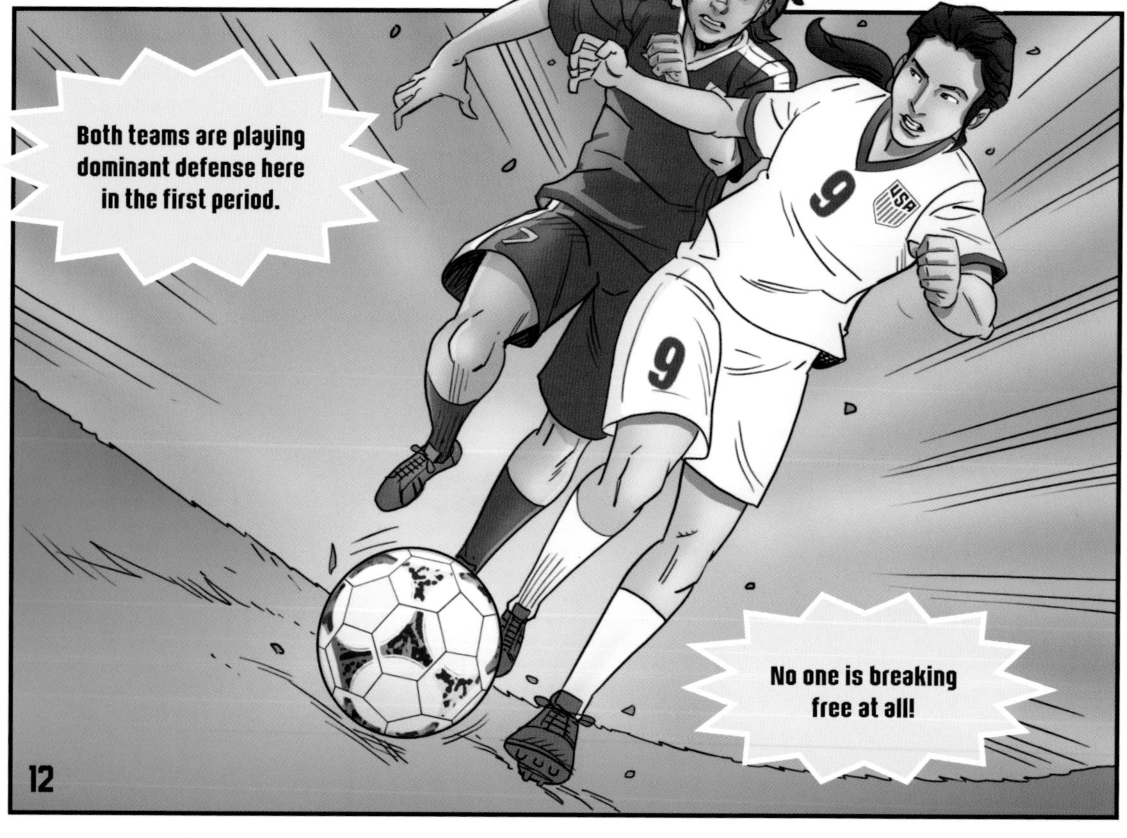
Both teams are playing dominant defense here in the first period.
No one is breaking free at all!

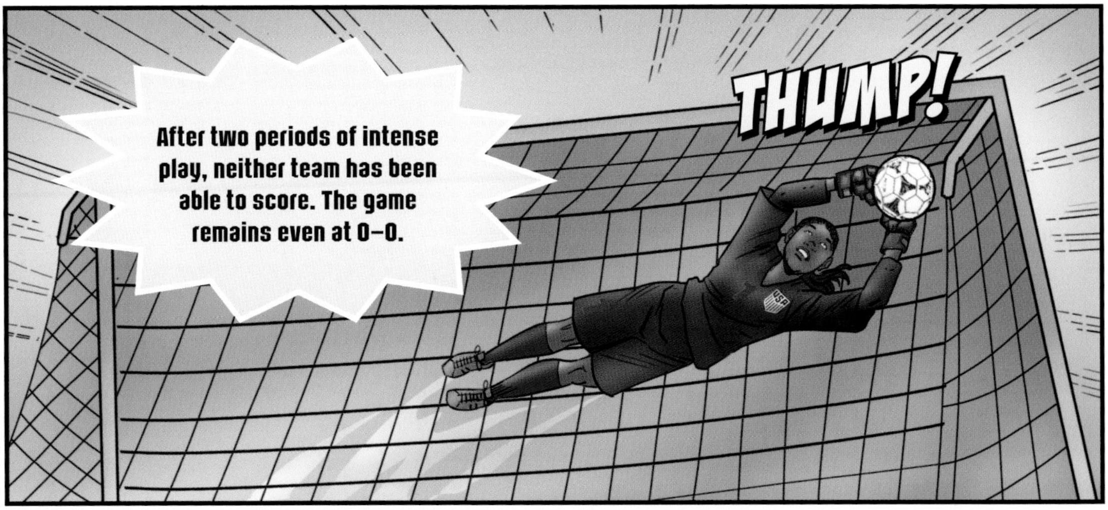
After two periods of intense play, neither team has been able to score. The game remains even at 0–0.
THUMP!

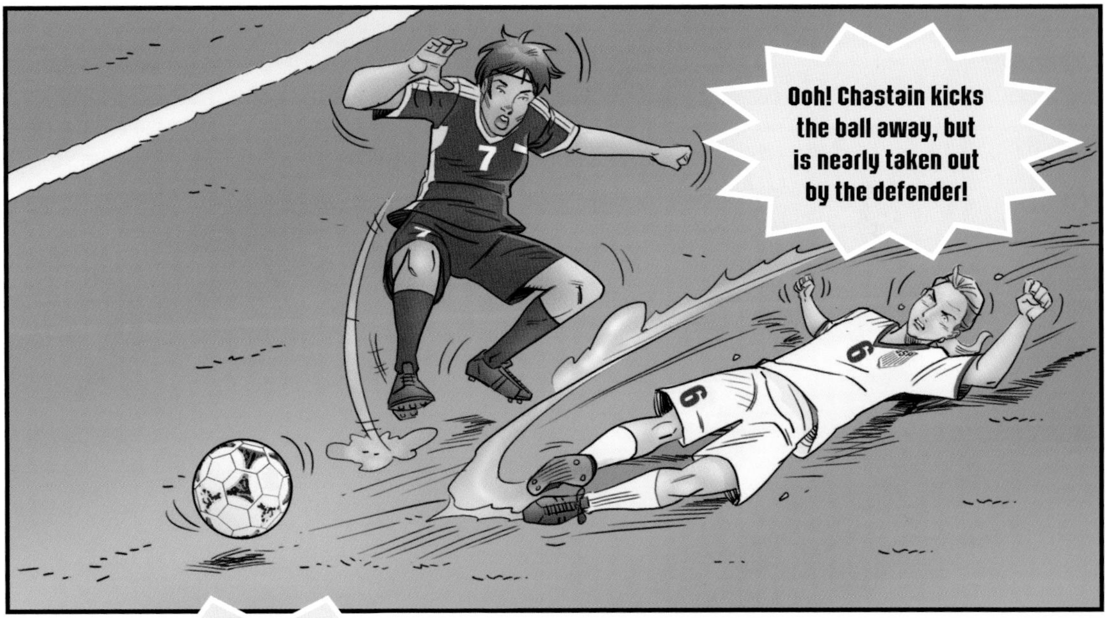
Ooh! Chastain kicks the ball away, but is nearly taken out by the defender!

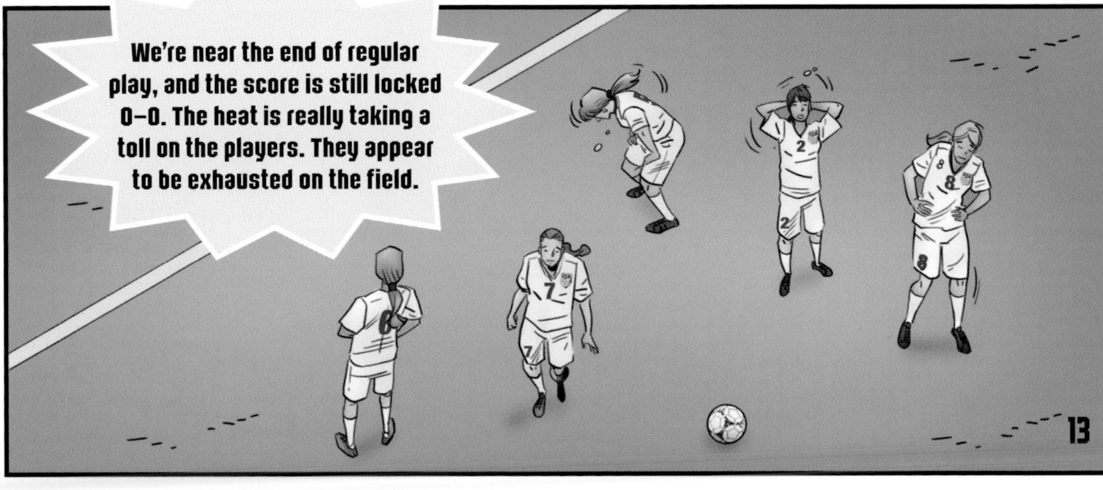
We're near the end of regular play, and the score is still locked 0–0. The heat is really taking a toll on the players. They appear to be exhausted on the field.

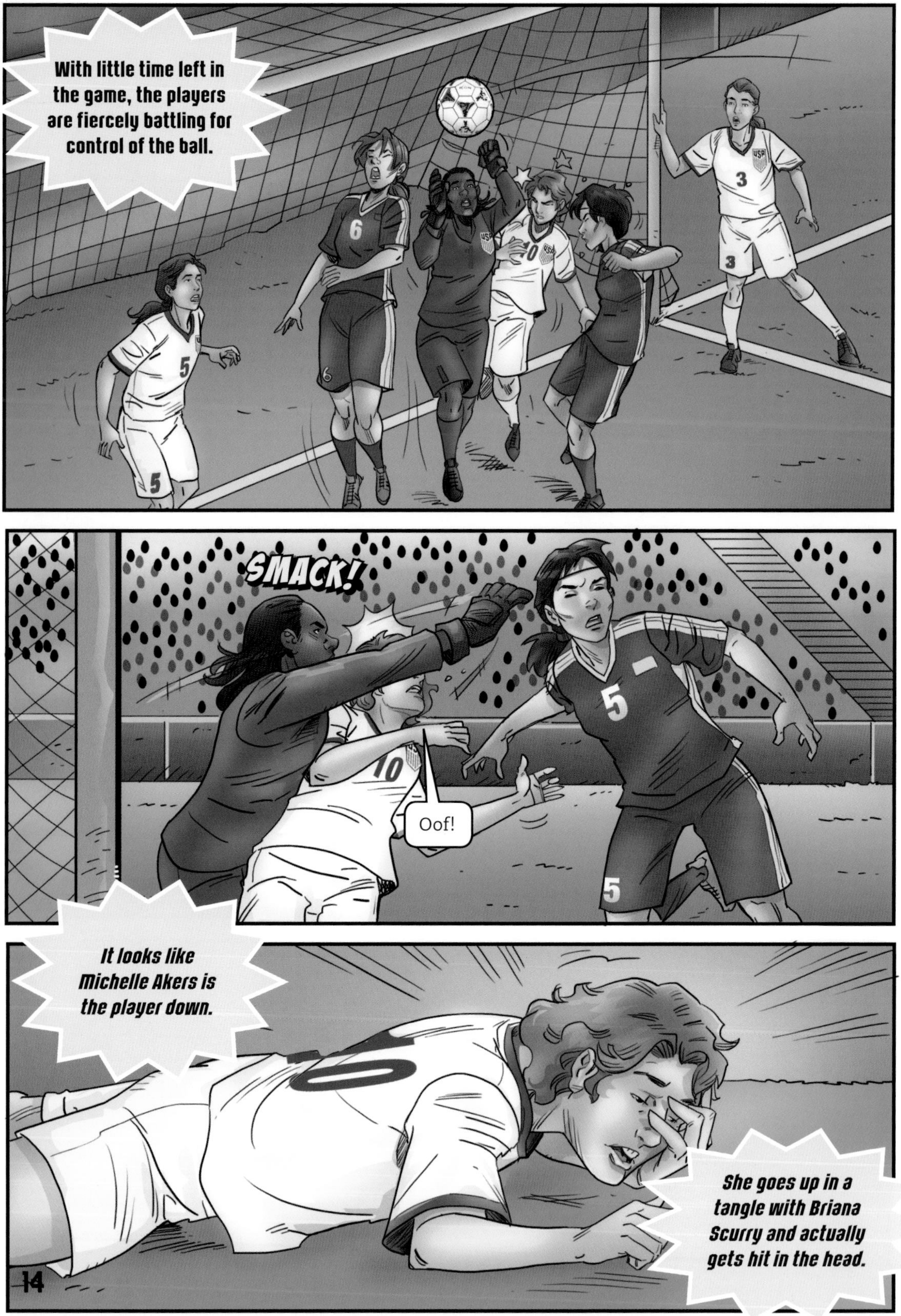
With little time left in the game, the players are fiercely battling for control of the ball.
SMACK!
Oof!
It looks like Michelle Akers is the player down.
She goes up in a tangle with Briana Scurry and actually gets hit in the head.

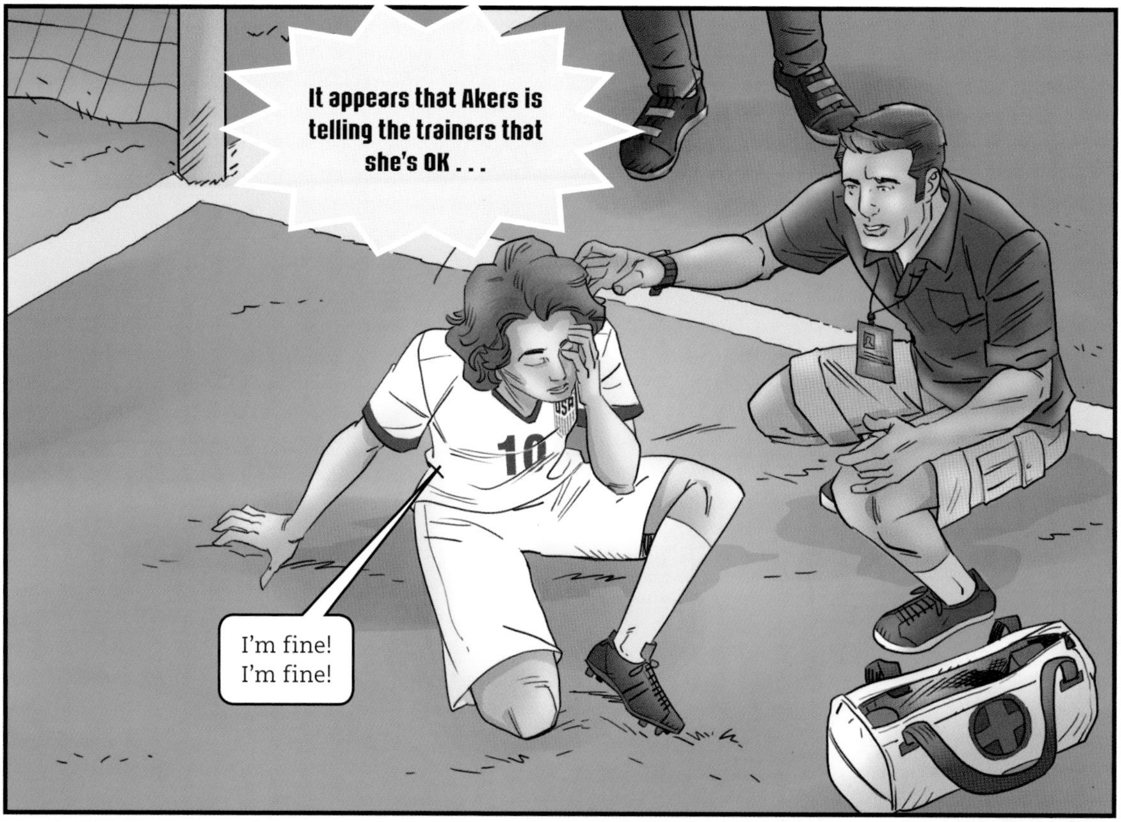
It appears that Akers is telling the trainers that she's OK . . .
I'm fine! I'm fine!

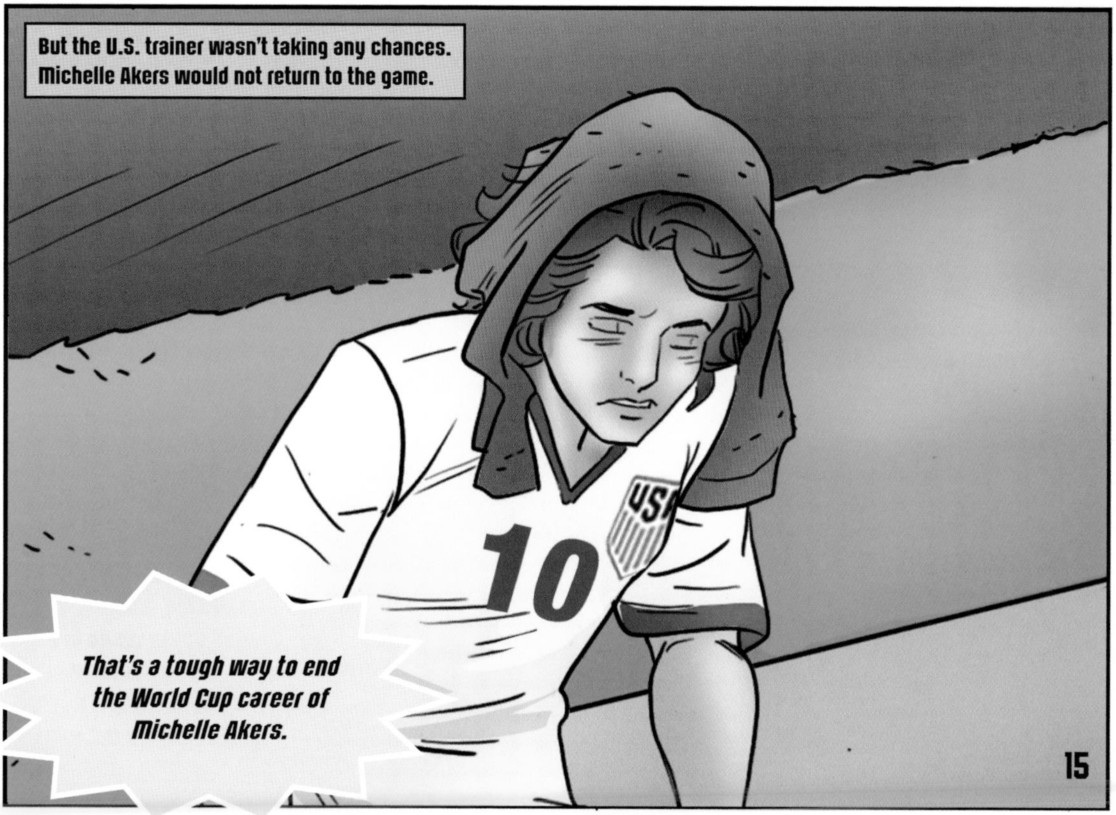
But the U.S. trainer wasn't taking any chances. Michelle Akers would not return to the game.
That's a tough way to end the World Cup career of Michelle Akers.

DEADLOCKED IN OT

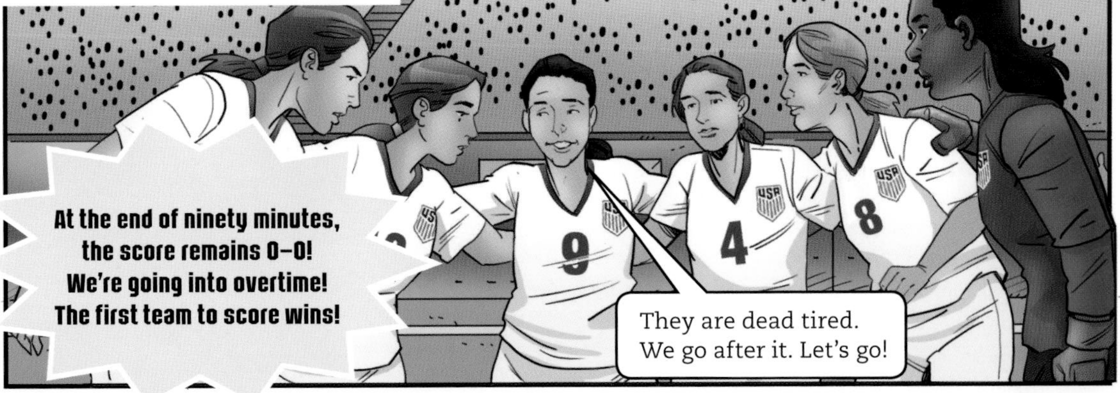

At the end of ninety minutes, the score remains 0–0! We're going into overtime! The first team to score wins!
They are dead tired. We go after it. Let's go!

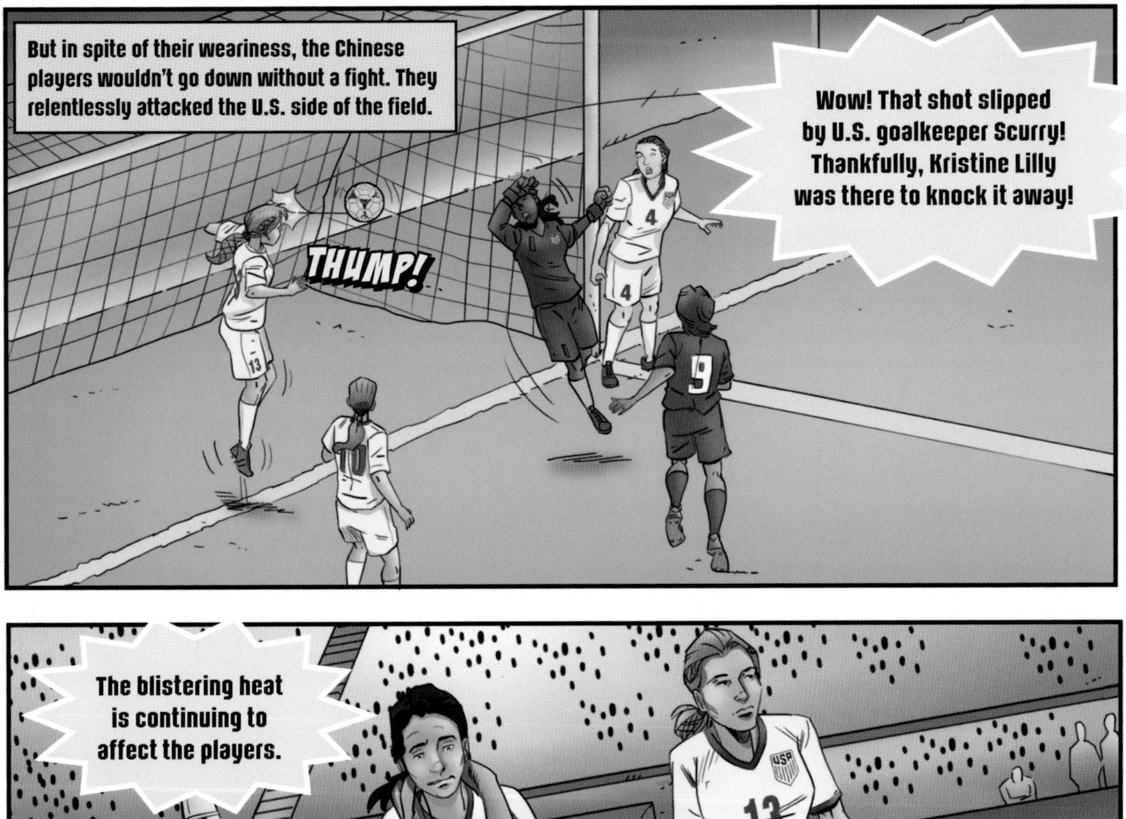

But in spite of their weariness, the Chinese players wouldn't go down without a fight. They relentlessly attacked the U.S. side of the field.
THUMP!
Wow! That shot slipped by U.S. goalkeeper Scurry! Thankfully, Kristine Lilly was there to knock it away!

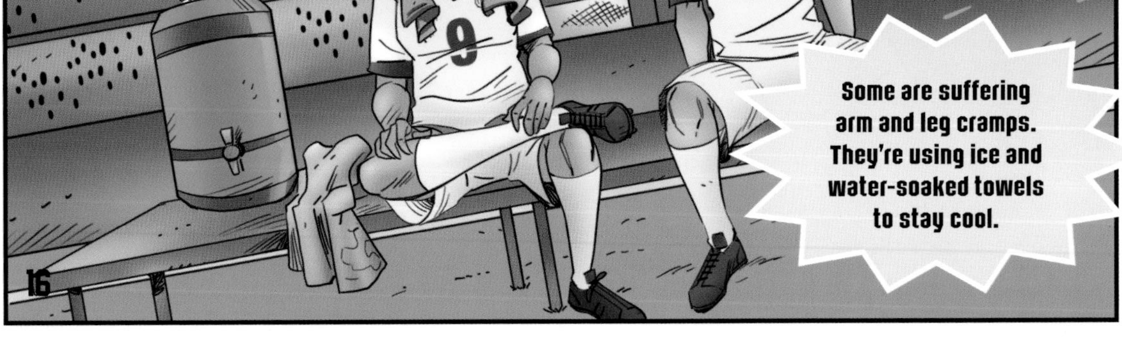

The blistering heat is continuing to affect the players.
Some are suffering arm and leg cramps. They're using ice and water-soaked towels to stay cool.

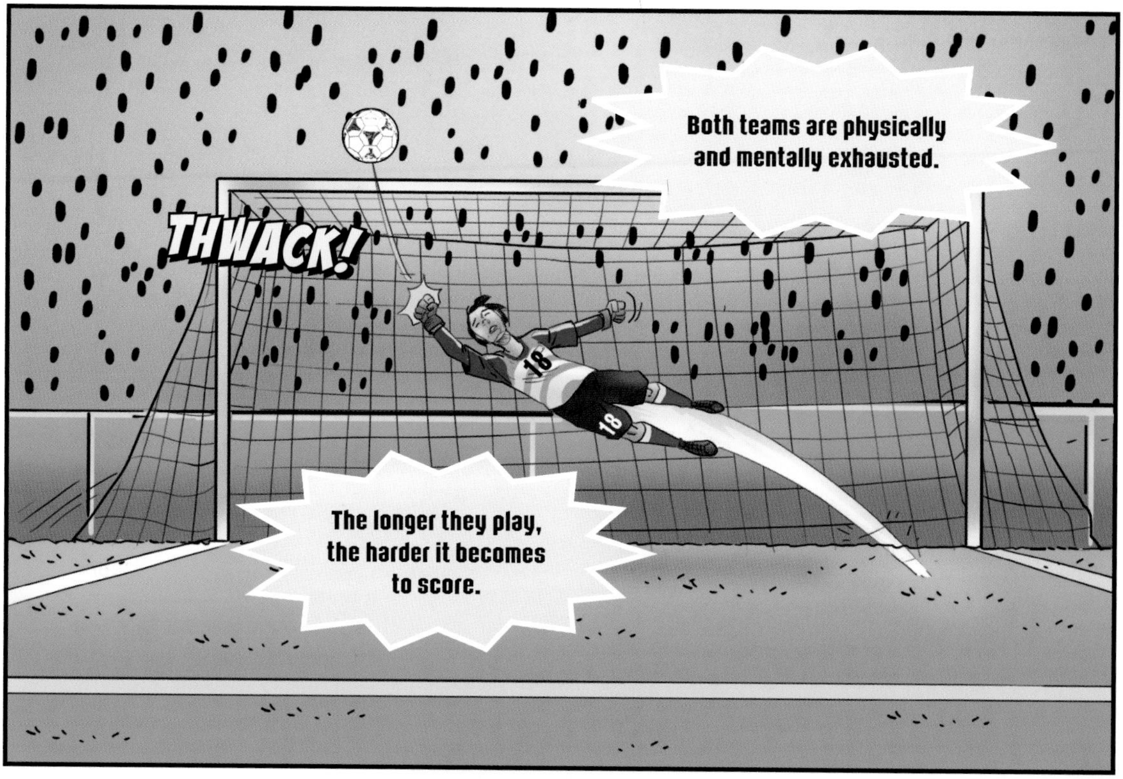
Both teams are physically and mentally exhausted.
THWACK!
The longer they play, the harder it becomes to score.

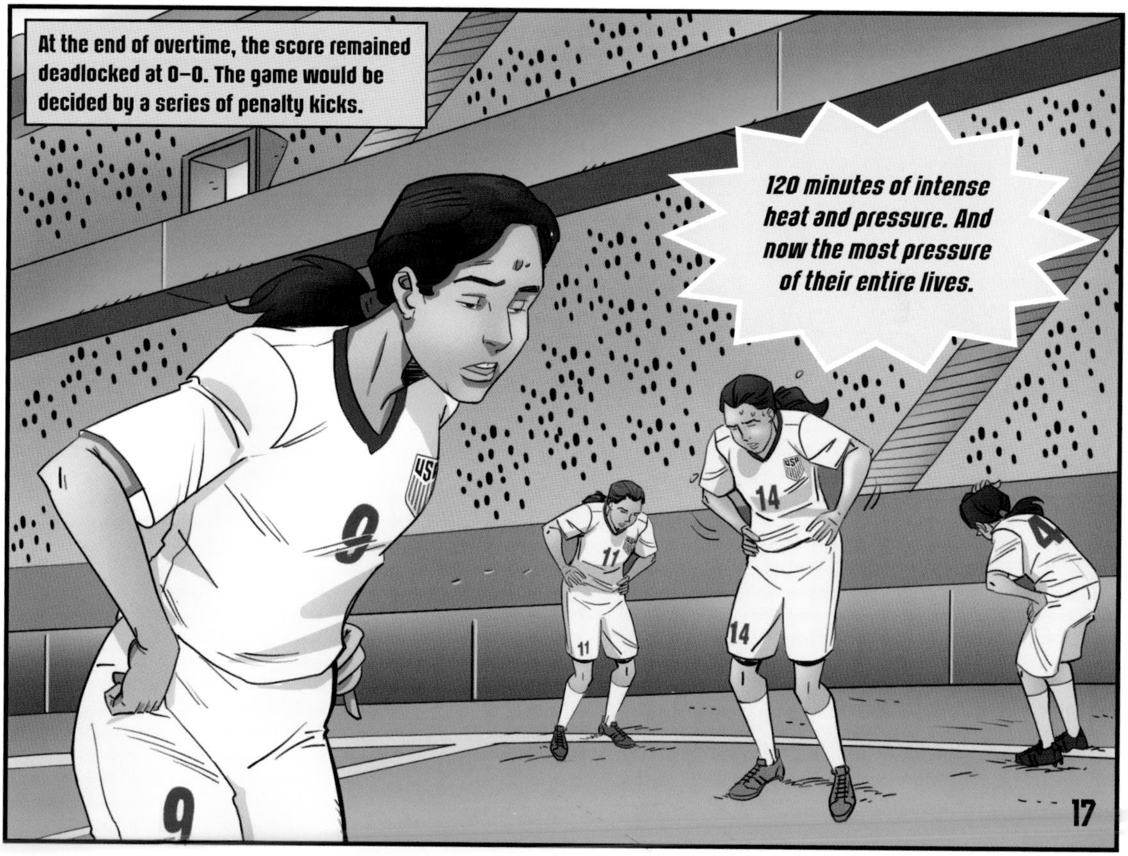
At the end of overtime, the score remained deadlocked at 0–0. The game would be decided by a series of penalty kicks.
120 minutes of intense heat and pressure. And now the most pressure of their entire lives.

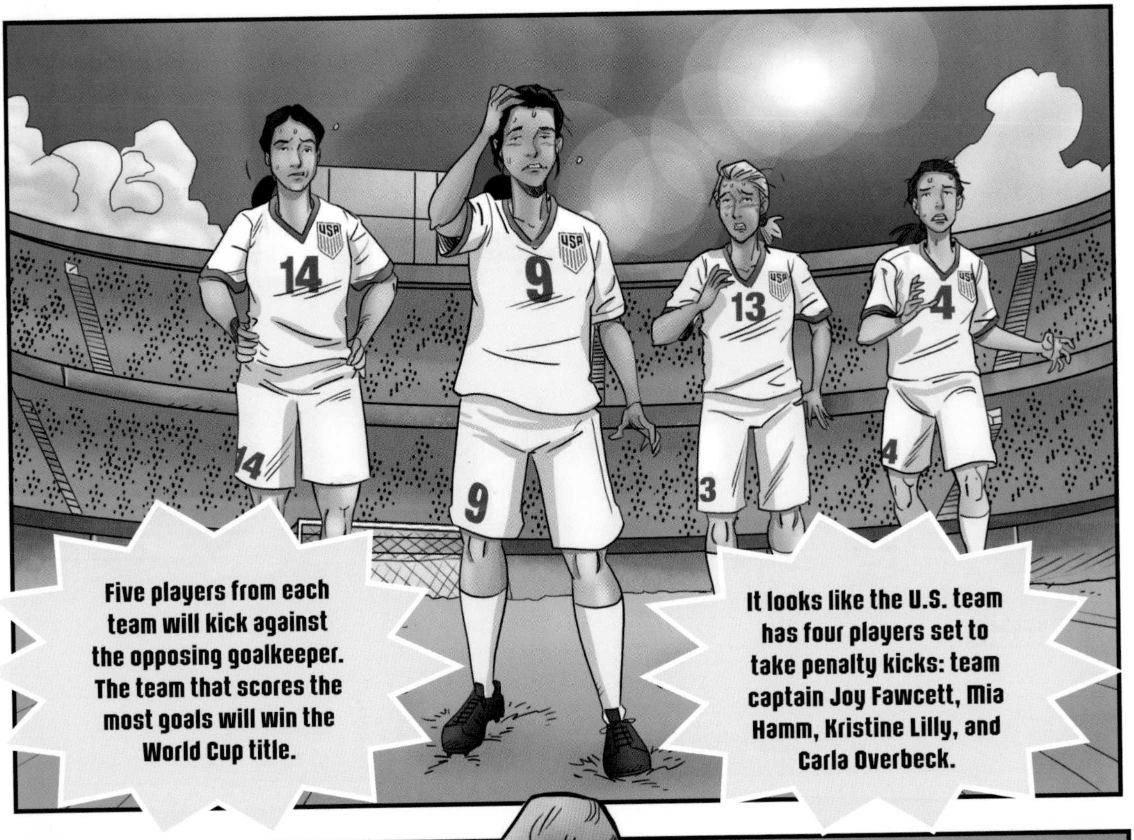
Five players from each team will kick against the opposing goalkeeper. The team that scores the most goals will win the World Cup title.
It looks like the U.S. team has four players set to take penalty kicks: team captain Joy Fawcett, Mia Hamm, Kristine Lilly, and Carla Overbeck.

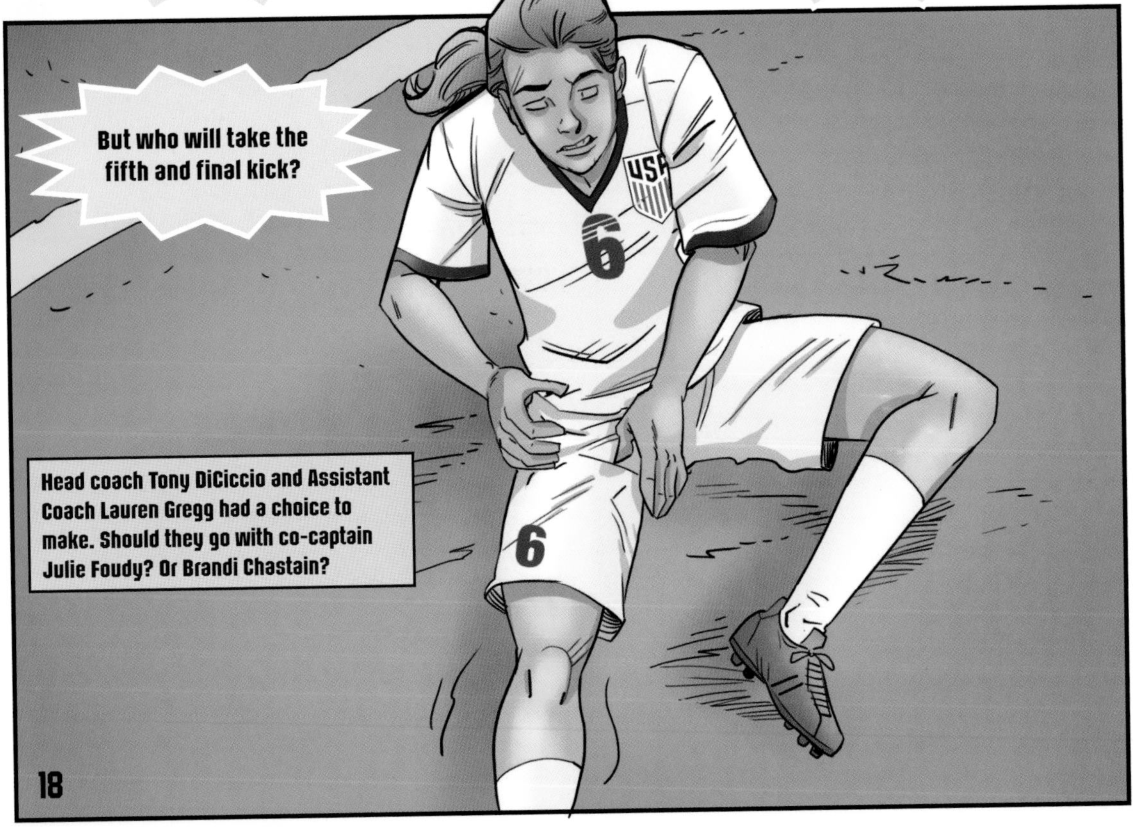
But who will take the fifth and final kick?
Head coach Tony DiCiccio and Assistant Coach Lauren Gregg had a choice to make. Should they go with co-captain Julie Foudy? Or Brandi Chastain?

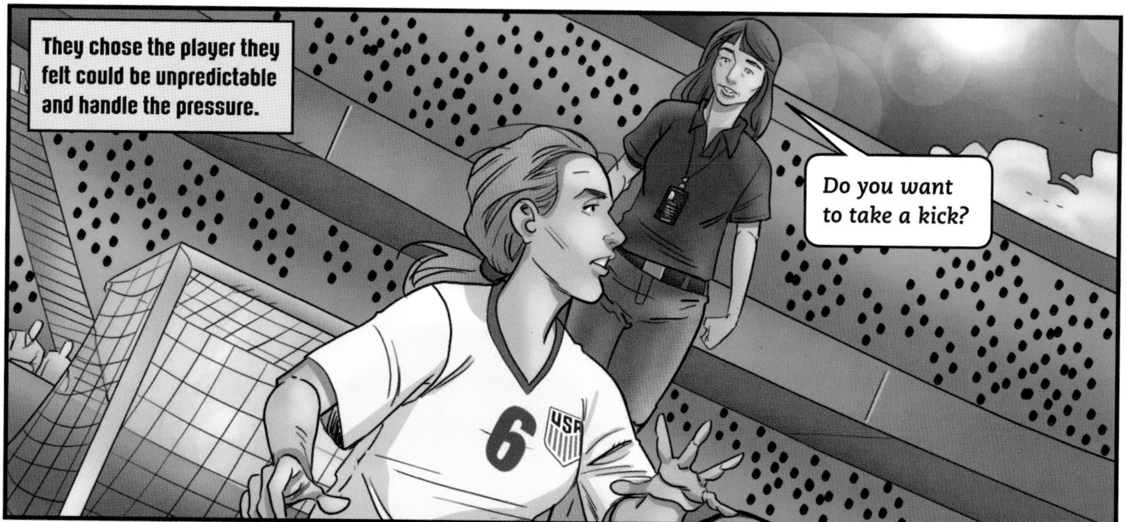
They chose the player they felt could be unpredictable and handle the pressure.
Do you want to take a kick?

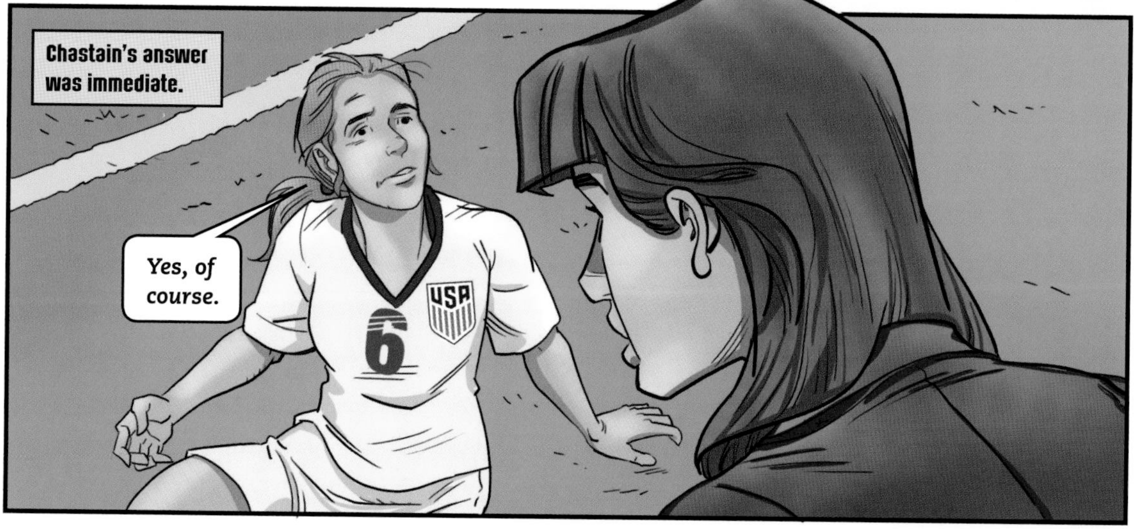
Chastain's answer was immediate.
Yes, of course.

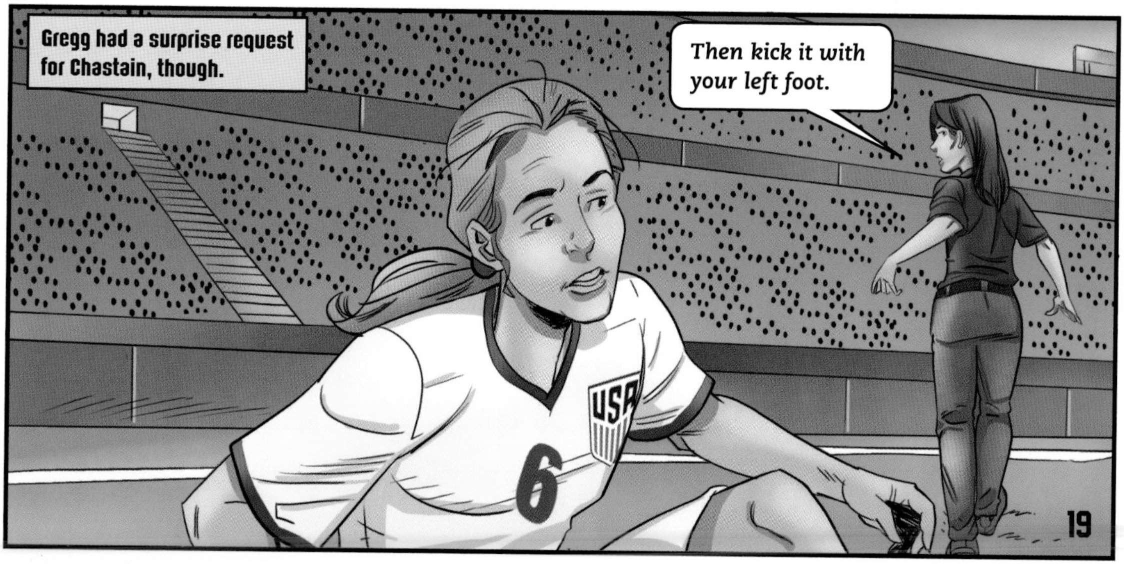
Gregg had a surprise request for Chastain, though.
Then kick it with your left foot.

SHOWDOWN AT THE NETS

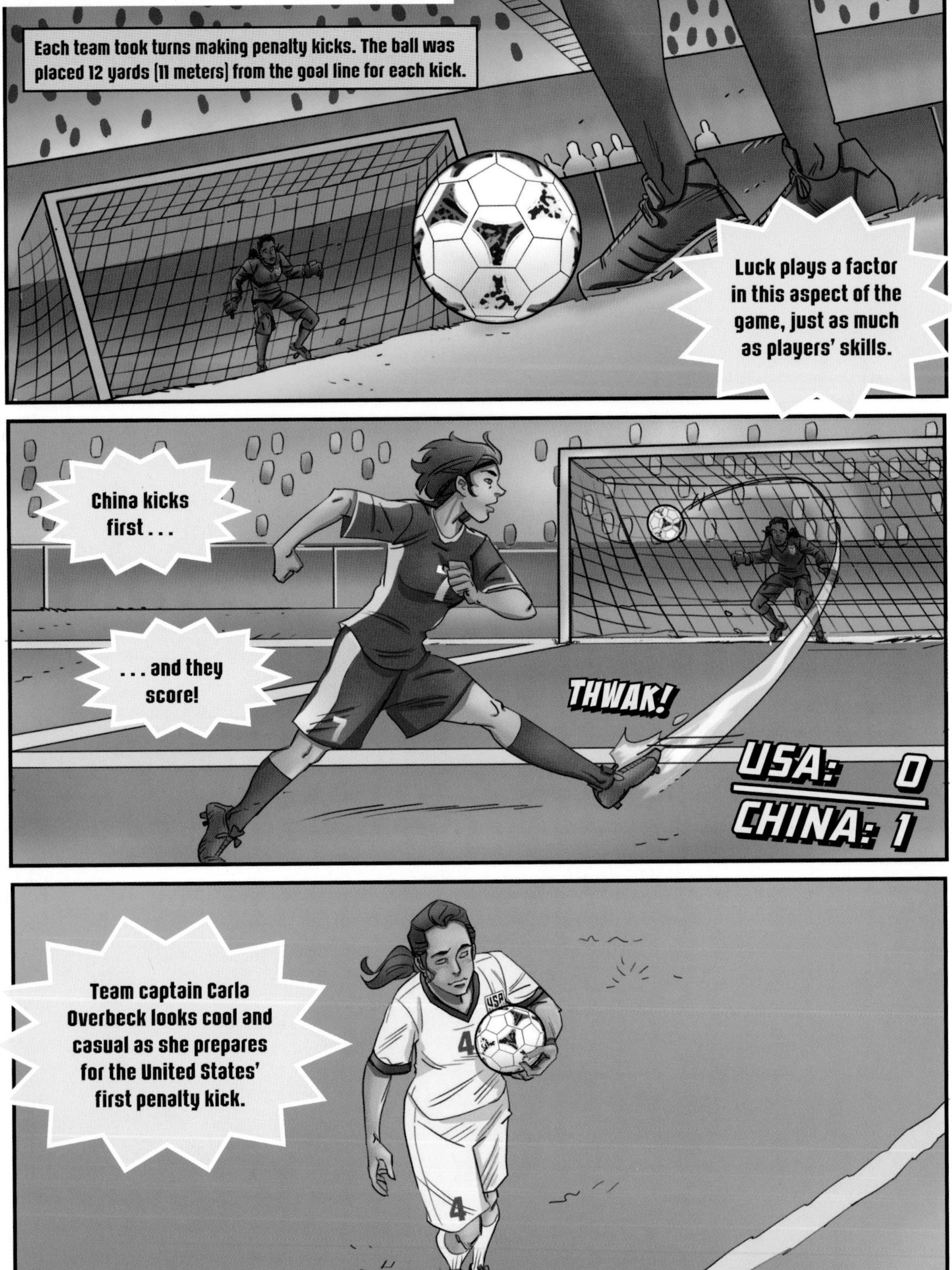

Each team took turns making penalty kicks. The ball was placed 12 yards (11 meters) from the goal line for each kick.
Luck plays a factor in this aspect of the game, just as much as players' skills.
China kicks first . . .
. . . and they score!
THWAK!
USA: 0
CHINA: 1
Team captain Carla Overbeck looks cool and casual as she prepares for the United States' first penalty kick.

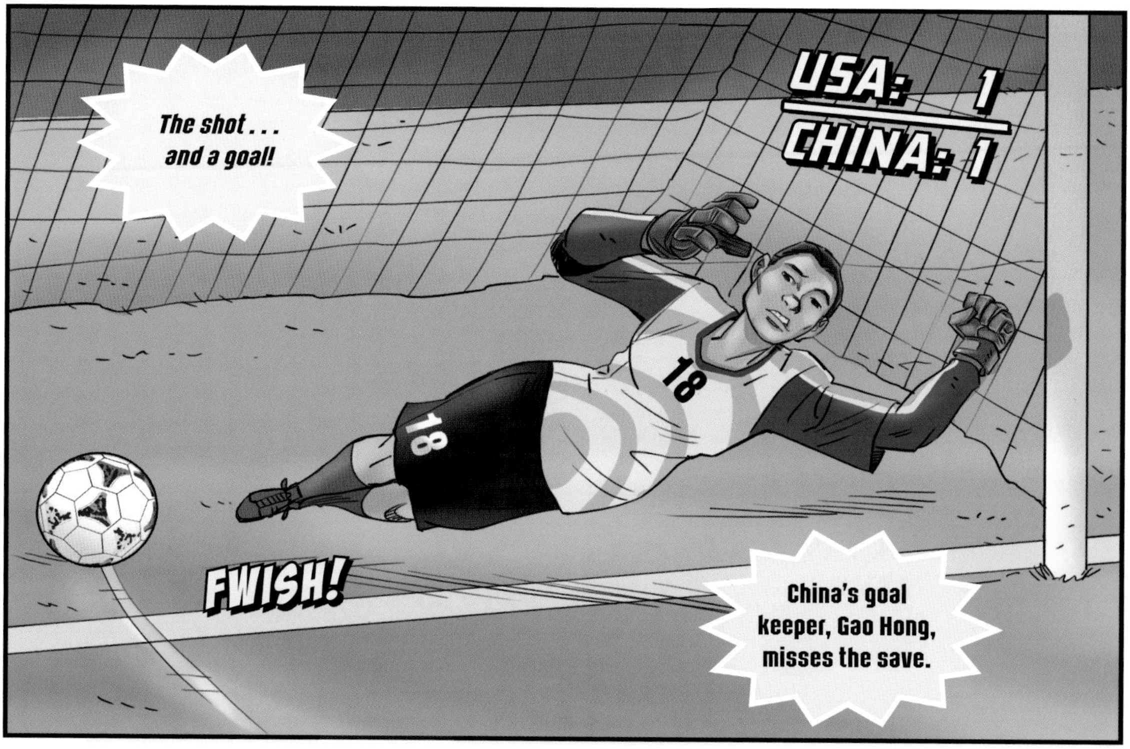
The shot . . . and a goal!
USA: 1
CHINA: 1
FWISH!
China's goal keeper, Gao Hong, misses the save.

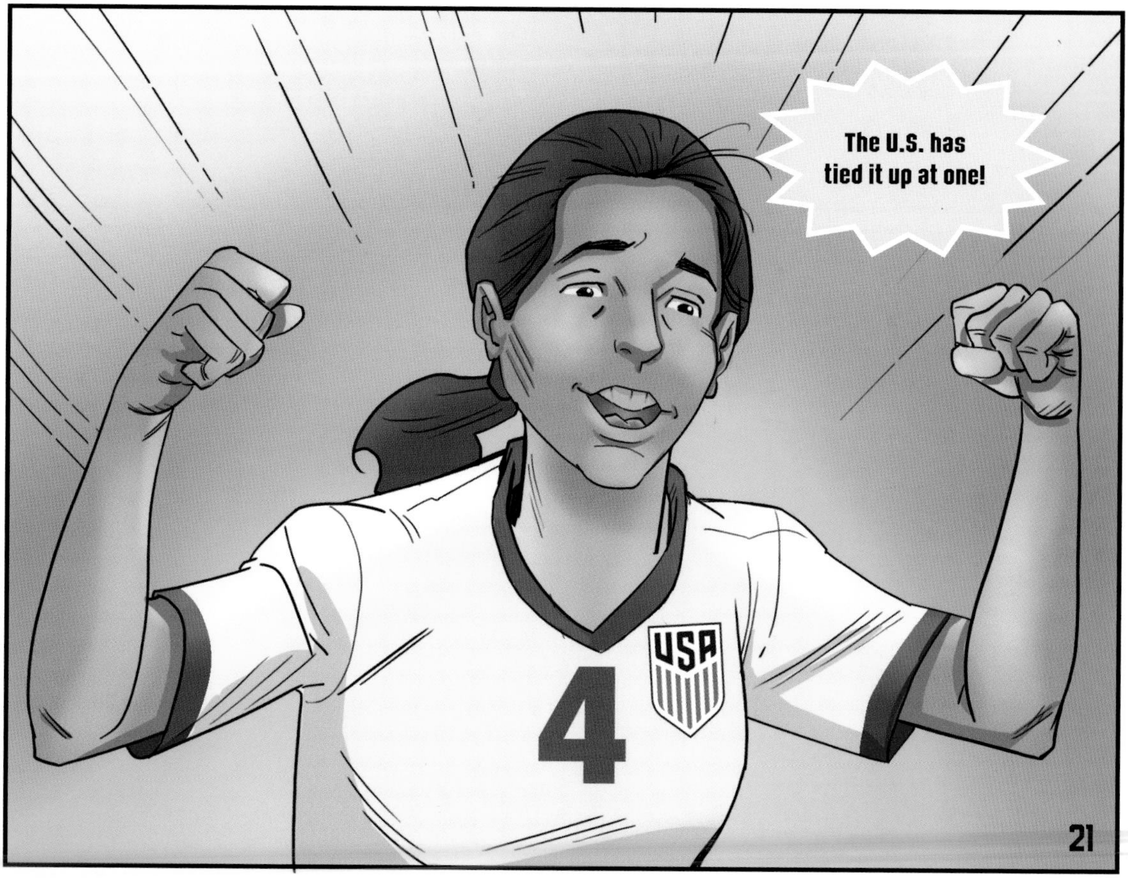
The U.S. has tied it up at one!
USA
4

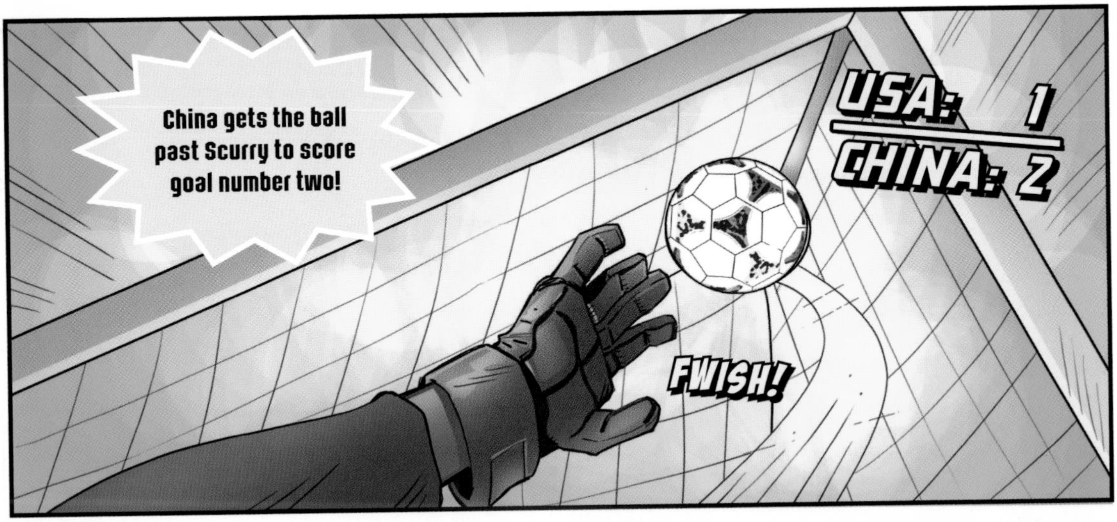
China gets the ball past Scurry to score goal number two!
USA: 1
CHINA: 2
FWISH!

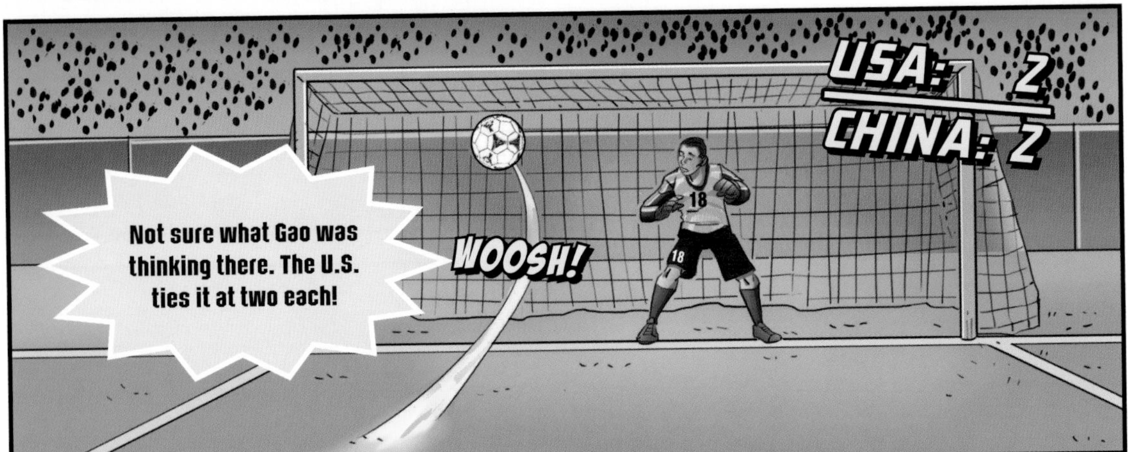
USA: 2
CHINA: 2
Not sure what Gao was thinking there. The U.S. ties it at two each!
WOOSH!

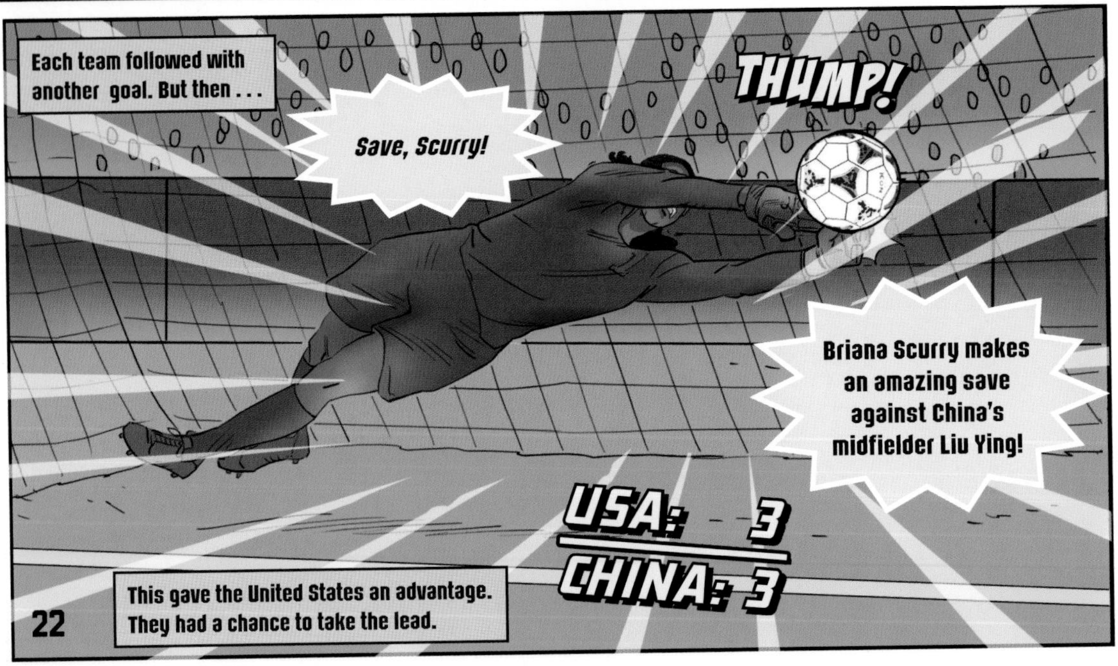
Each team followed with another goal. But then . . .
THUMP!
Save, Scurry!
Briana Scurry makes an amazing save against China's midfielder Liu Ying!
USA: 3
CHINA: 3
This gave the United States an advantage. They had a chance to take the lead.

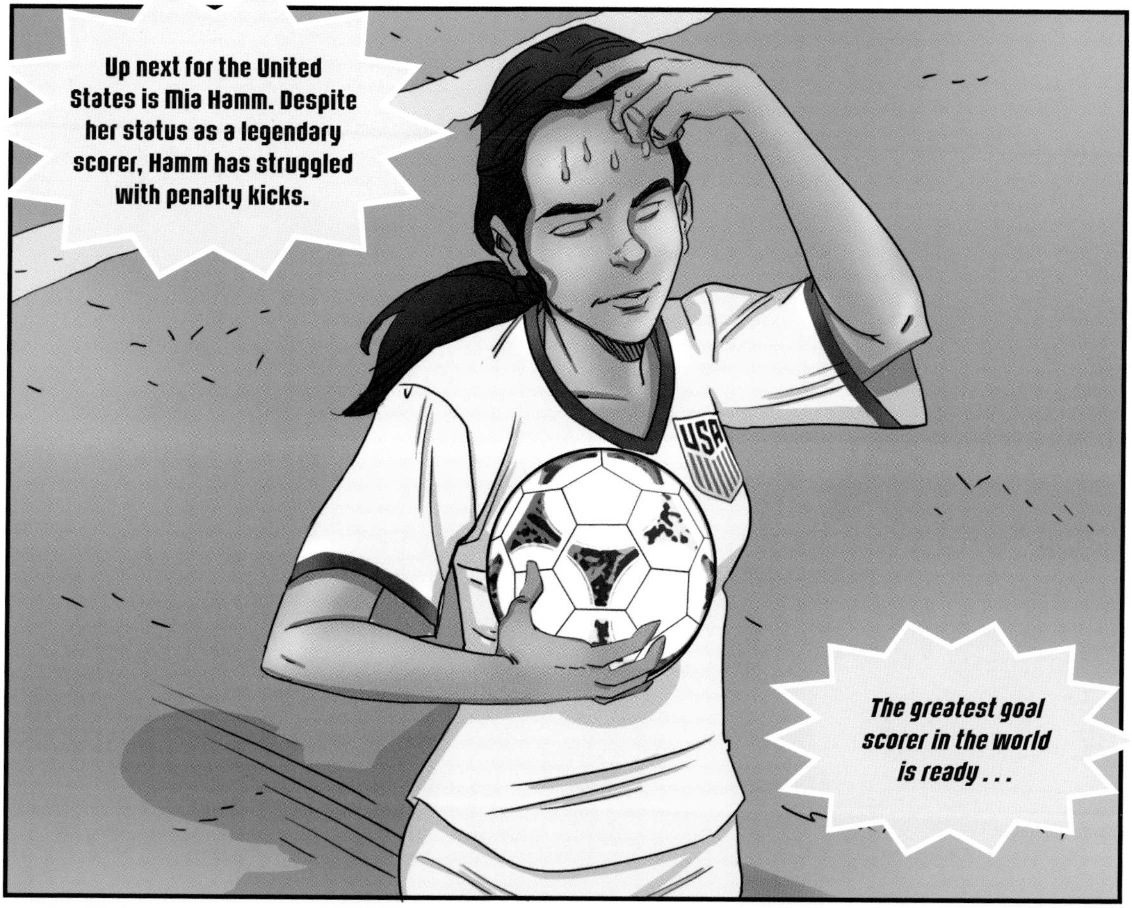
Up next for the United States is Mia Hamm. Despite her status as a legendary scorer, Hamm has struggled with penalty kicks.
The greatest goal scorer in the world is ready . . .

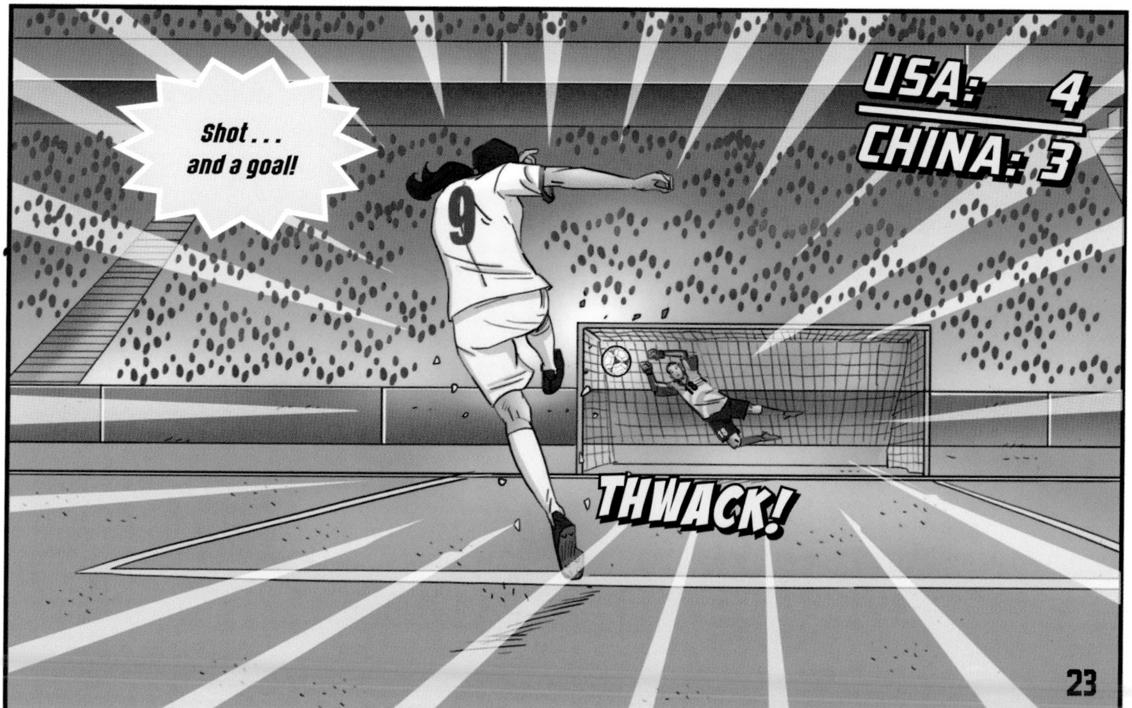
Shot . . . and a goal!
USA: 4
CHINA: 3
THWACK!

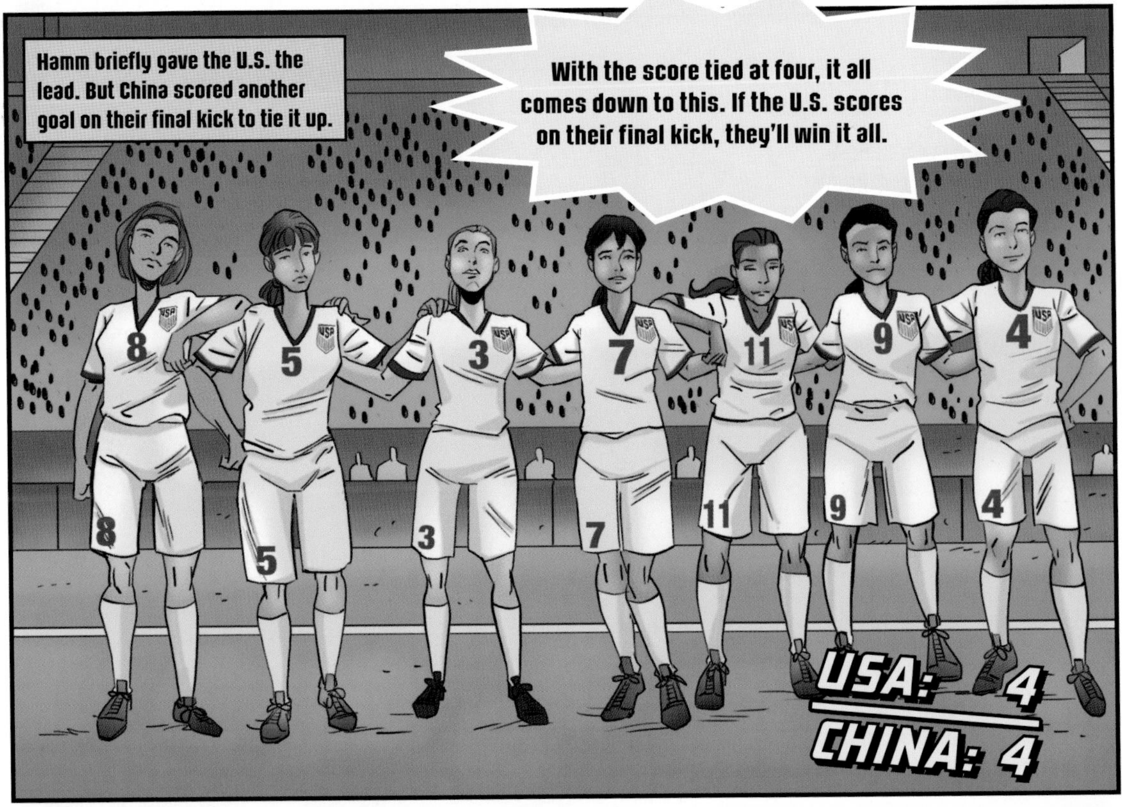
Hamm briefly gave the U.S. the lead. But China scored another goal on their final kick to tie it up.
With the score tied at four, it all comes down to this. If the U.S. scores on their final kick, they'll win it all.
USA: 4
CHINA: 4

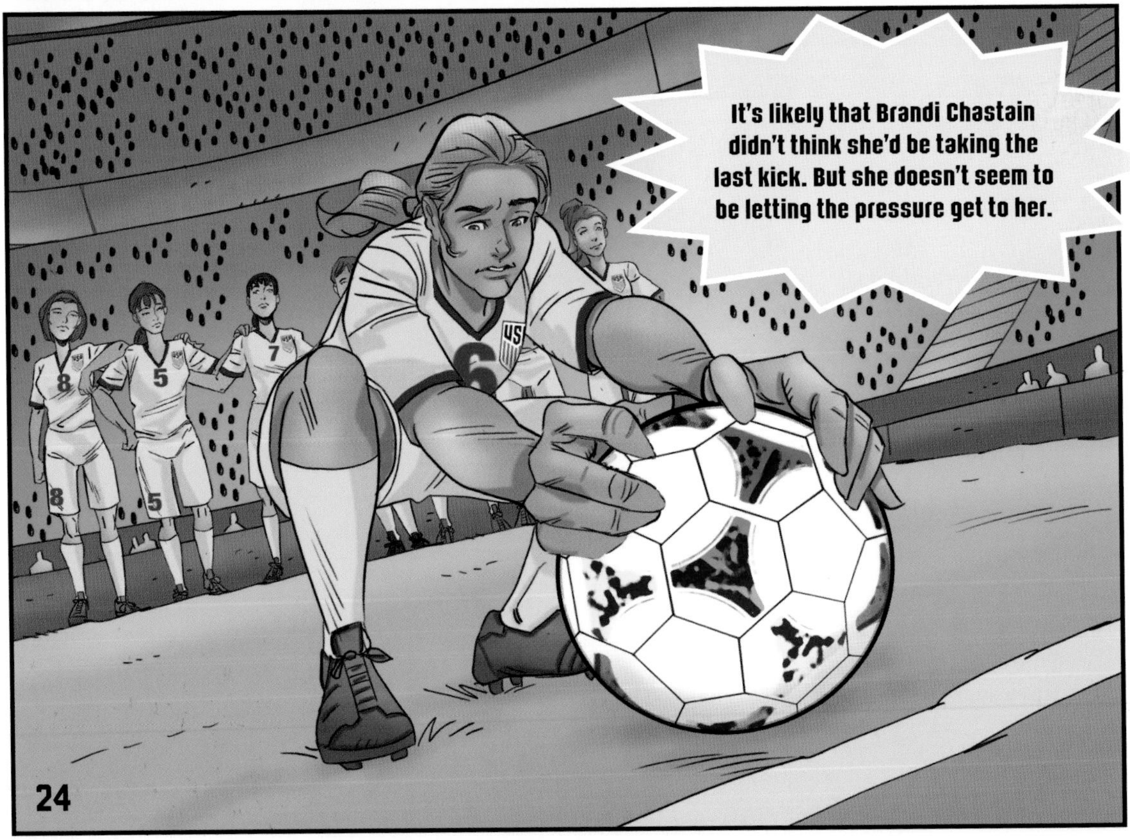
It's likely that Brandi Chastain didn't think she'd be taking the last kick. But she doesn't seem to be letting the pressure get to her.

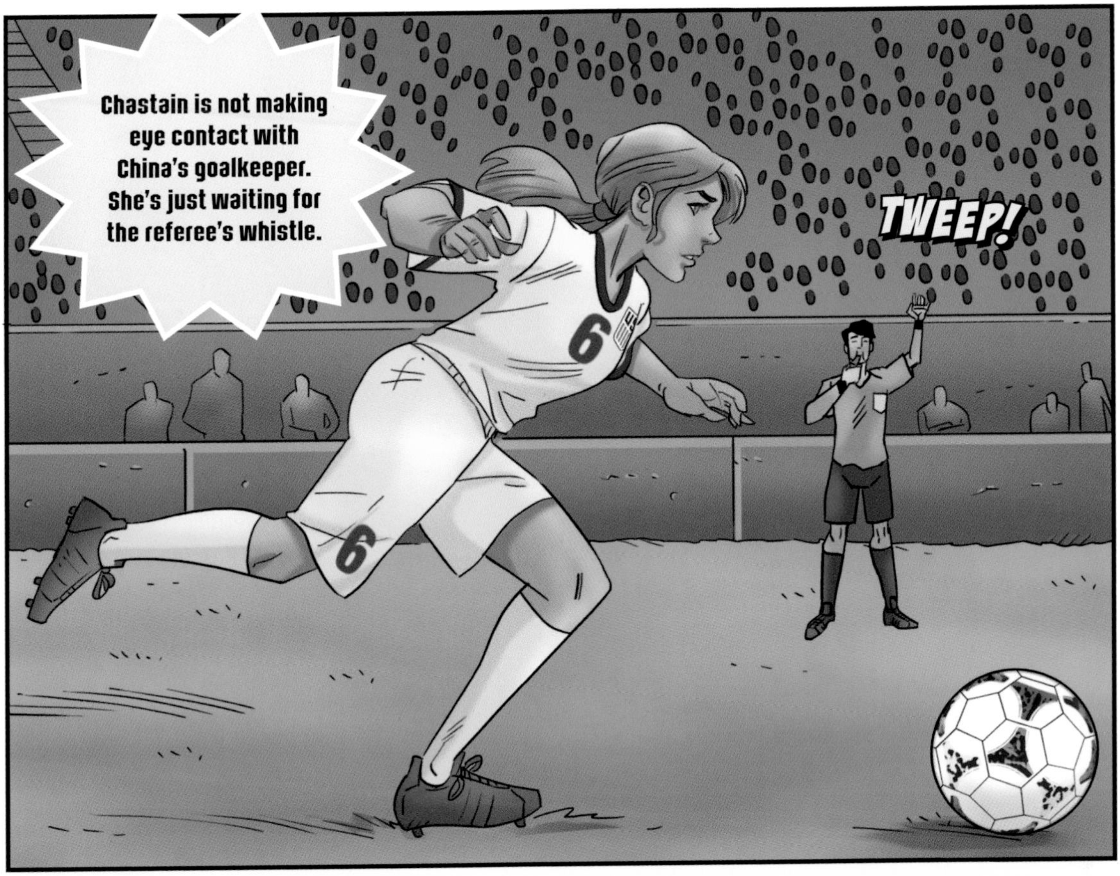
Chastain is not making eye contact with China's goalkeeper. She's just waiting for the referee's whistle.
TWEEP!

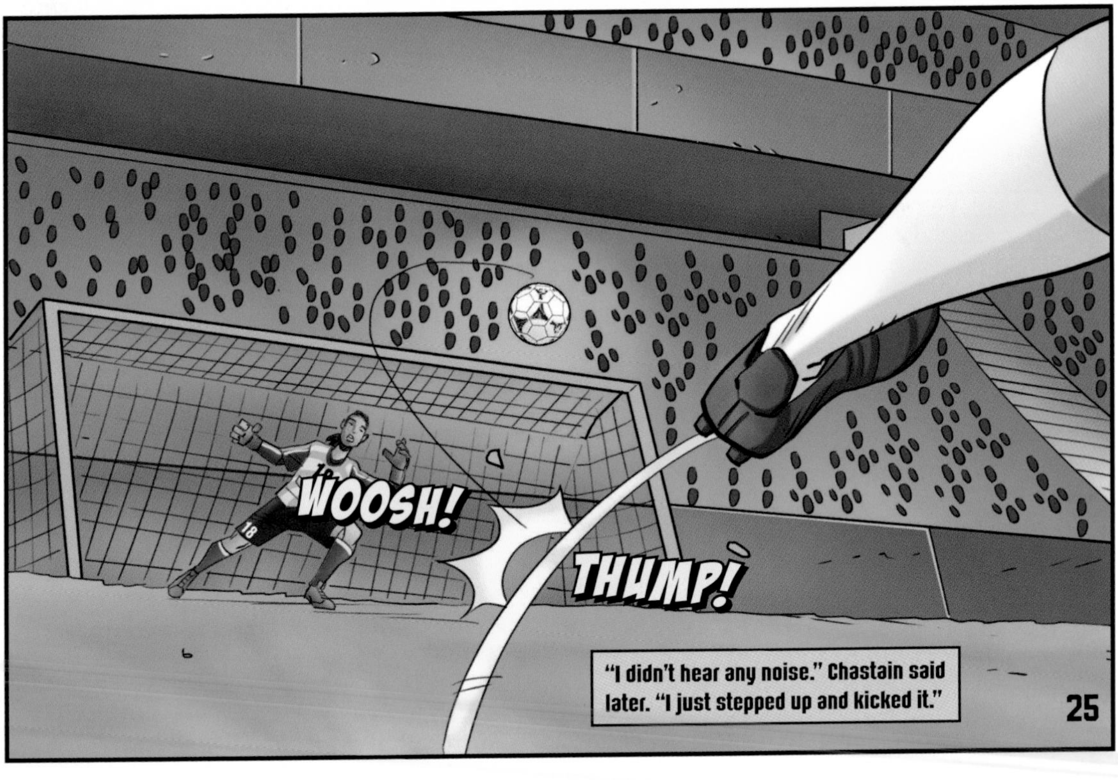
WOOSH!
THUMP!
"I didn't hear any noise." Chastain said later. "I just stepped up and kicked it."

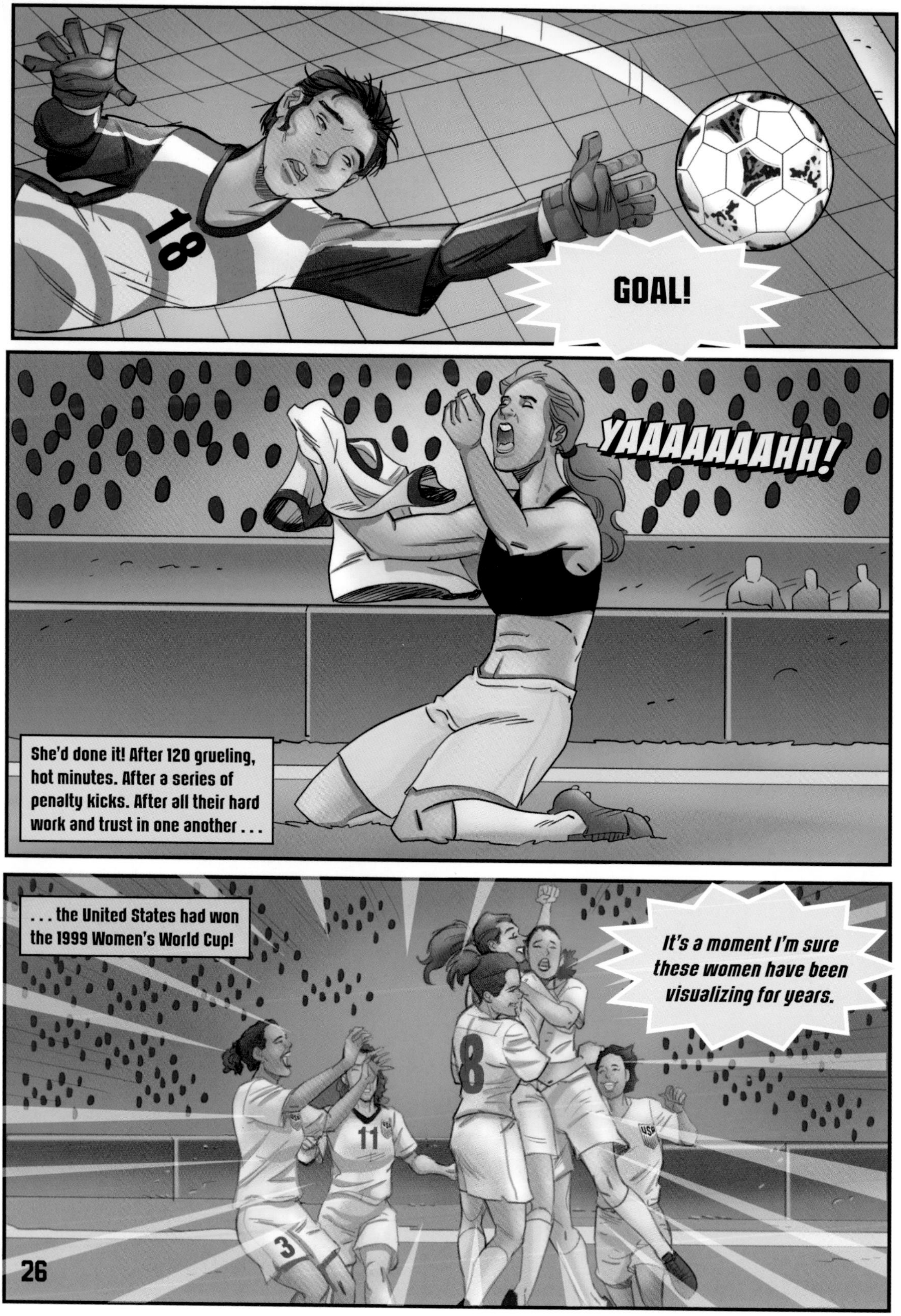
GOAL!
YAAAAAAAHH!
She'd done it! After 120 grueling, hot minutes. After a series of penalty kicks. After all their hard work and trust in one another . . .
. . . the United States had won the 1999 Women's World Cup!
It's a moment I'm sure these women have been visualizing for years.

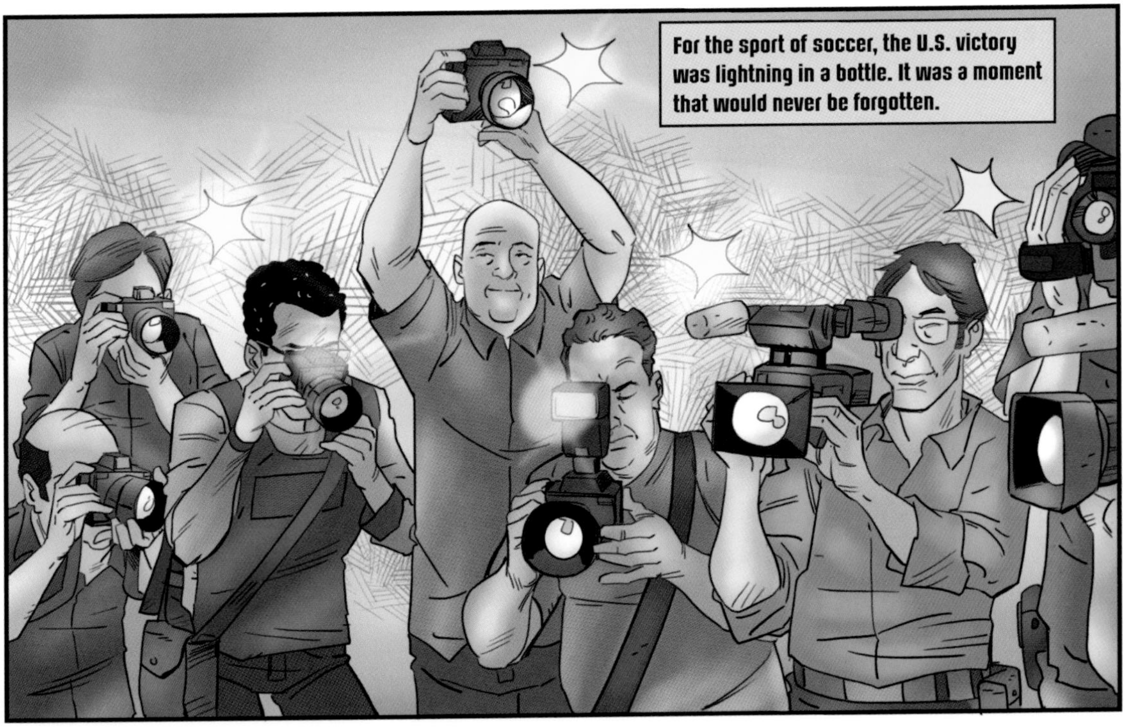
For the sport of soccer, the U.S. victory was lightning in a bottle. It was a moment that would never be forgotten.

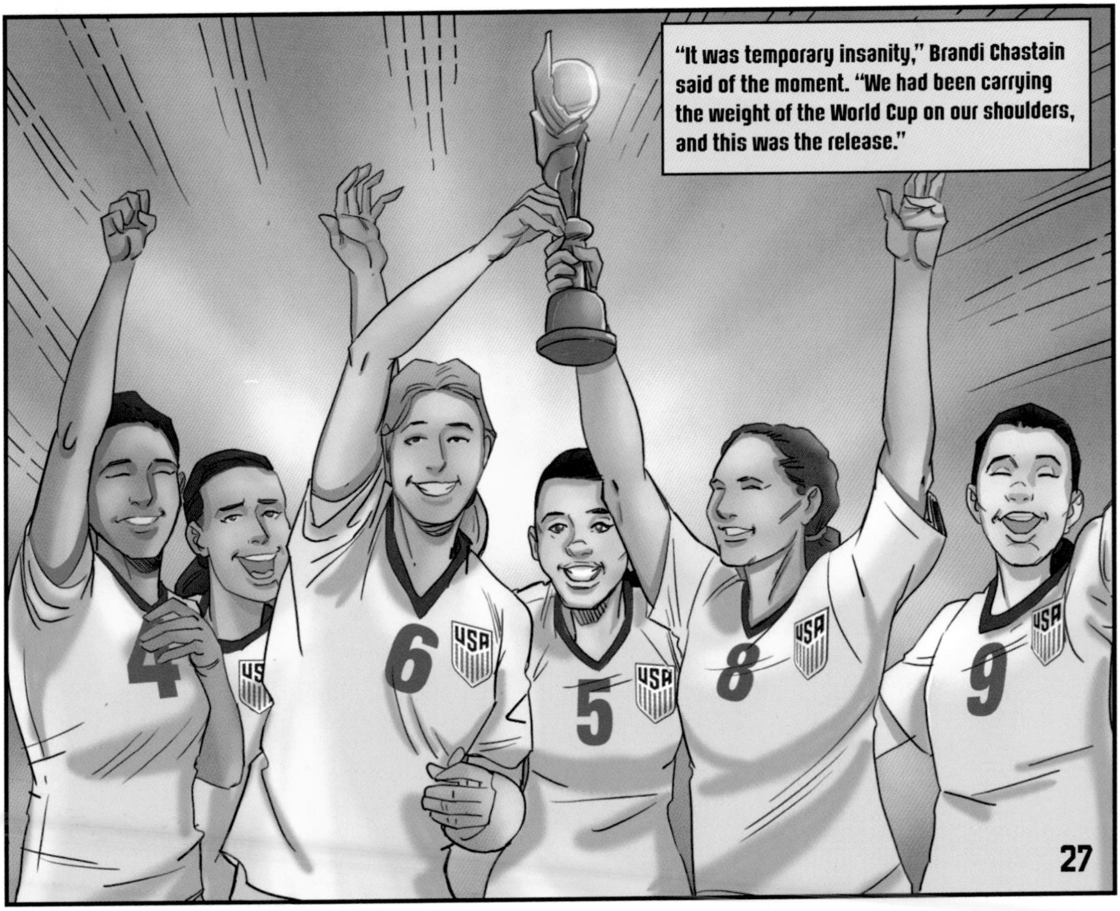
"It was temporary insanity," Brandi Chastain said of the moment. "We had been carrying the weight of the World Cup on our shoulders, and this was the release."

LASTING LEGACY

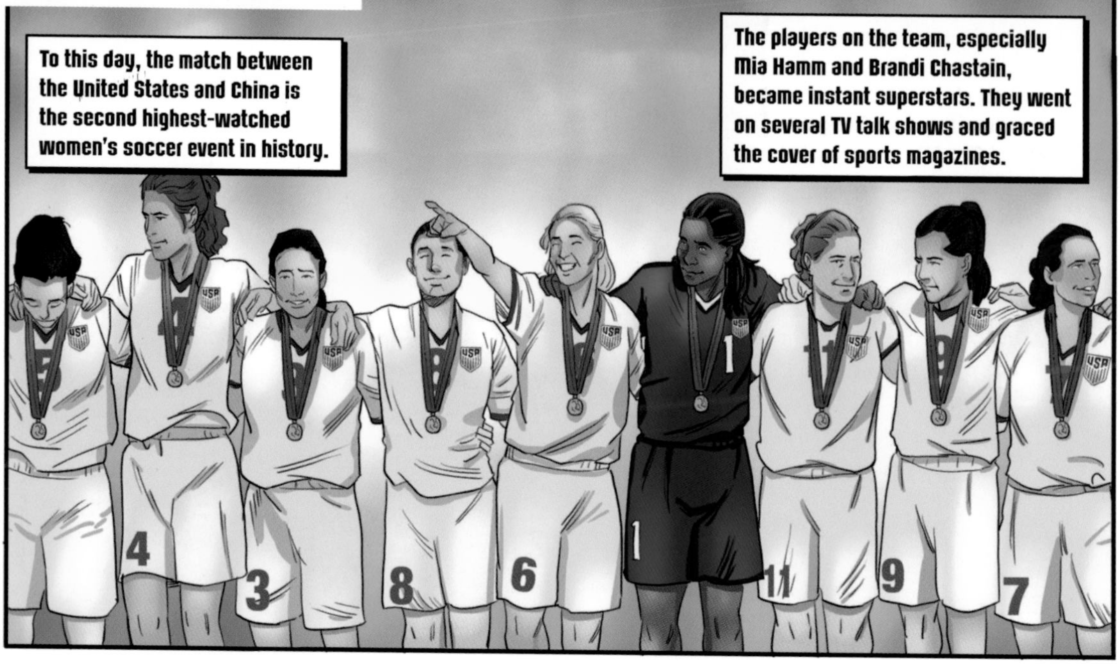
To this day, the match between the United States and China is the second highest-watched women's soccer event in history.
The players on the team, especially Mia Hamm and Brandi Chastain, became instant superstars. They went on several TV talk shows and graced the cover of sports magazines.

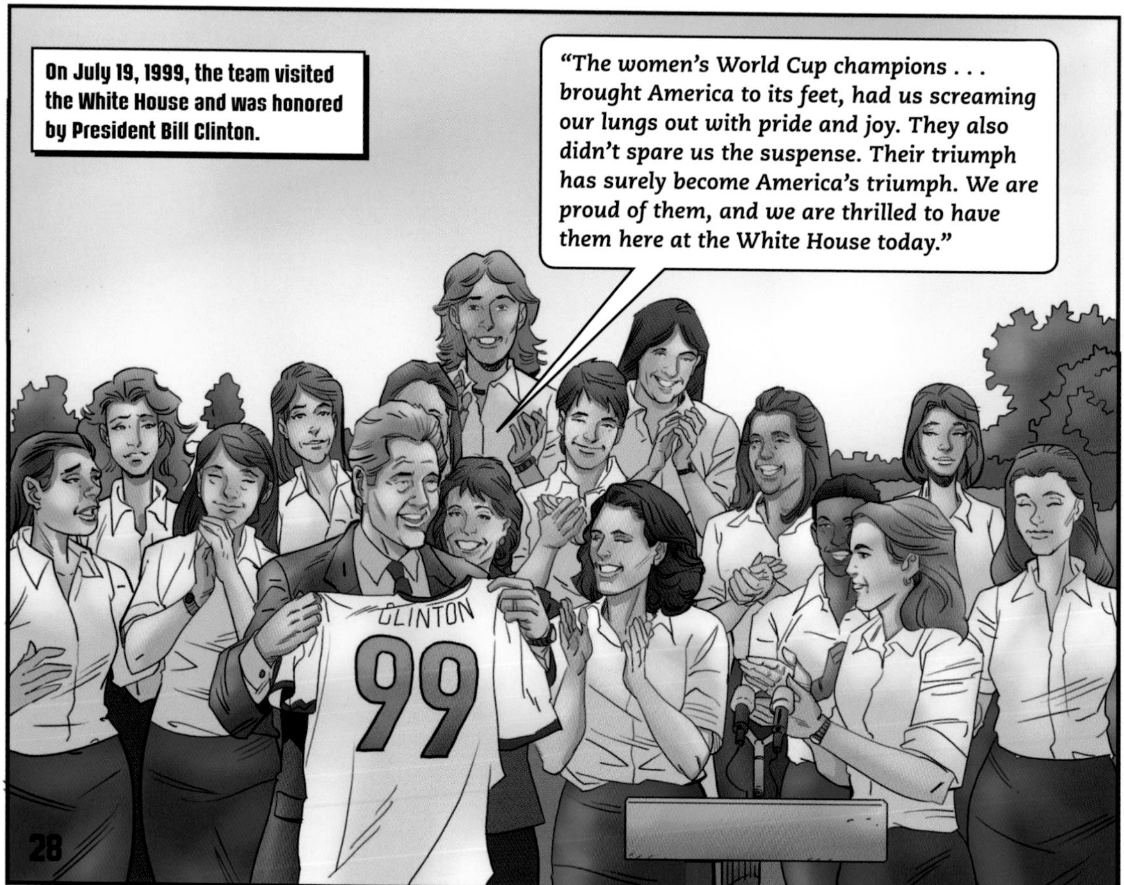
On July 19, 1999, the team visited the White House and was honored by President Bill Clinton.
"The women's World Cup champions . . . brought America to its feet, had us screaming our lungs out with pride and joy. They also didn't spare us the suspense. Their triumph has surely become America's triumph. We are proud of them, and we are thrilled to have them here at the White House today."
CLINTON
99

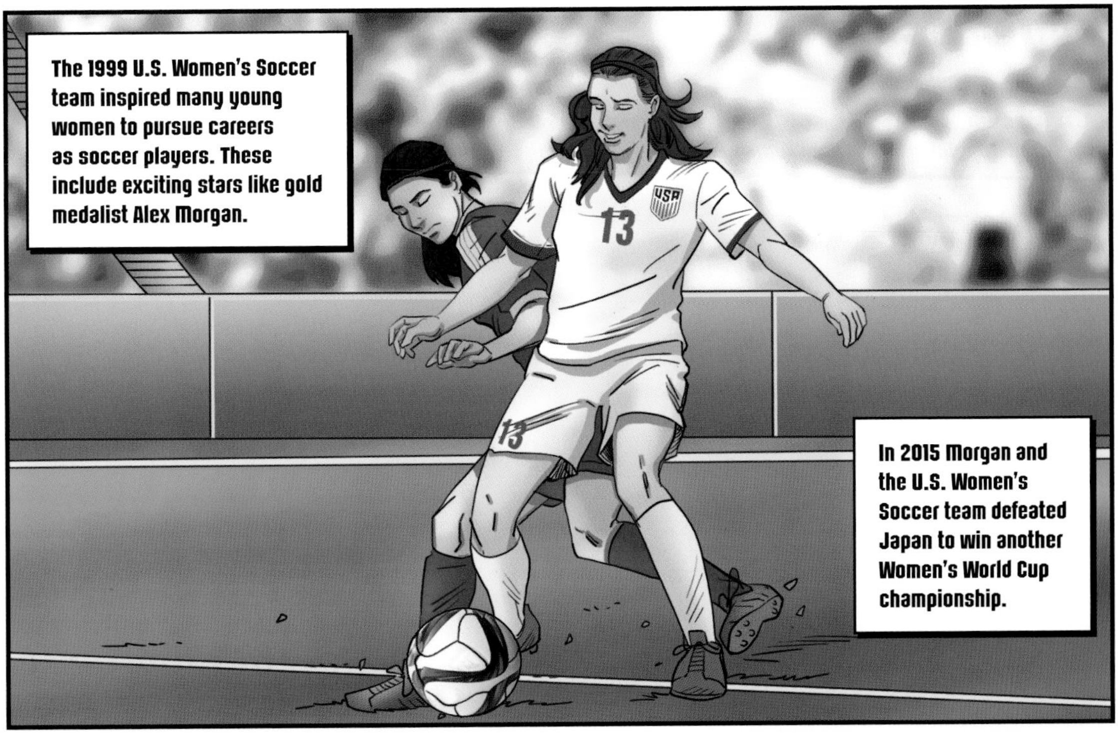
The 1999 U.S. Women's Soccer team inspired many young women to pursue careers as soccer players. These include exciting stars like gold medalist Alex Morgan.
In 2015 Morgan and the U.S. Women's Soccer team defeated Japan to win another Women's World Cup championship.

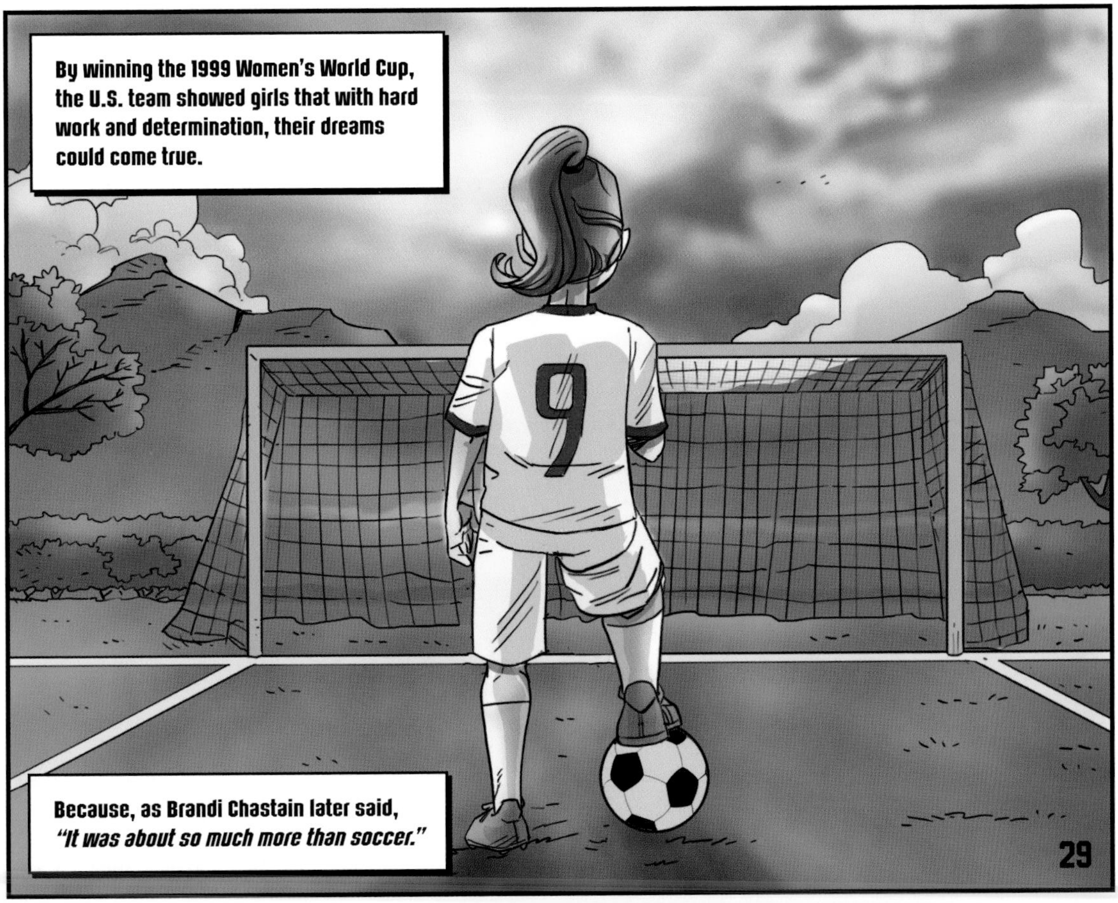
By winning the 1999 Women's World Cup, the U.S. team showed girls that with hard work and determination, their dreams could come true.
Because, as Brandi Chastain later said, *"It was about so much more than soccer."*

GLOSSARY

advantage (ad-VAN-tij)—something that is helpful or useful

creed (KREED)—a statement of basic beliefs

confident (KON-fi-duhnt)—sure of oneself

dominant (DOM-uh-nuhnt)—powerful or controlling, especially during a competition

exhibition match (ek-suh-BI-shuhn MACH)—a match played only for show and doesn't count toward team or player rankings

overtime (OH-vur-time)—an extra period played if the score is tied at the end of a game

penalty kick (PEN-uhl-tee KIK)—a free kick awarded to the offense when the defense commits a penalty

strategy (STRAT-uh-jee)—a plan to achieve a goal or win a competition

trainer (TRAY-nur)—a person who helps athletes get into condition to compete and treats injuries during a sports event

READ MORE

Hoena, Blake, with Omar Gonzalez. *Everything Soccer.* Everything Series. Washington, D.C.: National Geographic Society, 2014.

Savage, Jeff. *US Women's National Team: Soccer Champions.* Champion Soccer Clubs. Minneapolis: Lerner Publications, 2019.

Trusdell, Brian. *US Women Win the World Cup.* Greatest Events in Sports History. Minneapolis: ABDO Publishing, 2015.

CRITICAL THINKING QUESTIONS

- Star player Mia Hamm once said, ". . . the team, not the individual, is the ultimate champion." How do you think this applied to the 1999 U.S. Women's Soccer team?

- During the championship match the temperature soared to more than 100 degrees Fahrenheit (38 degrees Celcius.) Using examples from the text, explain how the heat affected the players and the game's outcome.

- Each player on the 1999 U.S. Women's Soccer team contributed to their victory. Write about a time when you helped a group or team achieve success.

INTERNET SITES

Use Facthound to find Internet sites related to this book.

Visit *www.facthound.com*

Just type in 9781543542202 and go.

 Super-cool stuff!

Check out projects, games and lots more at
www.capstonekids.com

INDEX